305.3   Berkowitz, Bob
BER
        What men won't tell
         you but women need
         to know

$16.45

WHAT MEN
WON'T TELL YOU
BUT WOMEN
NEED TO KNOW

WHAT MEN
WON'T TELL YOU
BUT WOMEN
NEED TO KNOW

Bob Berkowitz
with
Roger Gittines

WILLIAM MORROW
AND COMPANY, INC.
NEW YORK

Copyright © 1990 by Robert Berkowitz and Roger O. Gittines

All rights reserved. No part of this book may be reproduced or utilized in any form or by any means, electronic or mechanical, including photocopying, recording or by any information storage and retrieval system, without permission in writing from the Publisher. Inquiries should be addressed to Permissions Department, William Morrow and Company, Inc., 105 Madison Avenue, New York, N.Y. 10016.

Library of Congress Cataloging-in-Publication Data

Berkowitz, Bob.
  What men won't tell you but women need to know / Bob Berkowitz, Roger Gittines.
    p.   cm.
  ISBN 0-668-08779-5
  1. Men—United States—Psychology. 2. Masculinity (Psychology)—United States. I. Gittines, Roger. II Title.
HQ1090.3.B465   1990   89-12953
305.31—dc20   CIP

Printed in the United States of America

First Edition

1 2 3 4 5 6 7 8 9 10

BOOK DESIGN BY WILLIAM McCARTHY

To Merrilee.
My wife, my lover
and my best friend.

ACKNOWLEDGMENTS

My deepest thanks to Spencer Johnson and Warren Farrell, who encouraged and prodded me to write this book.

And I can't say enough about my literary agent, Margret McBride, and her senior editor, Winifred Golden. They are not only extremely professional, but showed a lot of care and love for this project.

Every author says he has the best editor in the business, but I really do. Adrian Zackheim and his terrific assistant, Pam Altschul, were a wonderful pain in the butt, to make sure that I gave them the best book I could. Thanks, guys.

Let me give special thanks to Steve Friedman, who as executive producer of *Today* gave me the opportunity to begin my great adventure as a men's reporter.

I can't possibly list all the people who shared their experiences, insights, and ideas with me. But there are a great number of people who gave a lot of time to this book. Here's a partial list: Merry Clark, Ted Hannah, Bonnie Hammer, Bernard Dornbusch, David Golden, Mark Lubin, John Flaherty, Beth Minardi, Gae Morris, Debra Benton, Jane Berger, Laurence Gross, Stephanie Longmire, Joann Ewalt, Teri Bronocco, Chris Harty, and Sally Stewart.

And let me thank my family: my wife, Merrilee; my

brother, Bill Berkowitz; my stepbrothers, Neal Newman and Harvey Rich; and my stepsister, Sandy Newman. Finally, a special acknowledgment to my parents. Some kids are lucky enough to have two good parents. I've been blessed with four great ones: my dad, Bernard Berkowitz; my late mother, Dee Rich; my stepmother, Mildred Newman; and my stepfather, Manny Rich.

They gave me the foundation of not only what it means to be a man, but to be a good man.

CONTENTS

Introduction   13
Chapter One   Men Are Different . . .   19
Chapter Two   The Basic Man   27
Chapter Three   The Open Man   41
Chapter Four   Ego Is Everything   59
Chapter Five   Big Sports   69
Chapter Six   You're Fired   77
Chapter Seven   Jerks "R" Us   81
Chapter Eight   Dating   91
Chapter Nine   Bald Spots   115
Chapter Ten   Teasers and Flirts   119
Chapter Eleven   Boys Just Want to Have Sex   127
Chapter Twelve   The "C" Word—*Commitment*   151
Chapter Thirteen   The Downside   167
Chapter Fourteen   His Cheating Heart   175
Chapter Fifteen   Word Play   187
Chapter Sixteen   Happily Ever After   195

WHAT MEN
WON'T TELL YOU
BUT WOMEN
NEED TO KNOW

INTRODUCTION

I

Hulking figures in Burberry trenchcoats follow me whenever I leave my apartment. The phone makes funny buzzing noises. I can tell that somebody has been reading all the junk mail (the return-reply cards are missing).

I think my cover has been blown. It's only a matter of time before they come for me.

They?—the members of a powerful secret cult. I've spent years investigating their strange rituals, and I'm just now beginning to break the code.

My only hope is to tell all before they silence me. Wait! I hear glass shattering. The lights have gone out. The screen of my word processor is blank. It's too late! They're here! *(gun shots; fade to black)*

So much for paranoid fantasies. Although men are a secret society, I don't have to worry about retribution for telling all—or as much as I understand—about the whats and whys and wherefores of half the human race. In fact, when I started to write this book, dozens of men agreed to help. They spent hours telling me about their lives and their loves, in the hope that women would gain a better understanding of what it is that makes them men.

The cooperation surprised me, because men have been traditionally reluctant to come out from behind the wall of silence. We hurt alone, hope alone, grieve and exult alone. But the willingness to "open up" a little suggests that men are beginning to outgrow the stereotype in which they find themselves trapped—the lonesome cowboy, the Lone Eagle, all the strong and silent warriors and hunters. Still, we're not very good at this thing the Russians call glasnost.

There are so many unanswered questions about men, and women have often been forced to turn to other women to fill in the blanks. Like American Kremlinologists reading Pravda and scanning stacks of satellite photos, women—reporters, psychologists, social scientists, and political reformers—have turned their research into books and magazine articles that examine men from almost every angle.

The basic assumption at the core of this book—a book about men written by a man—is that any study is only as good as its primary sources, and as a journalist I have been able to gain more insight and knowledge directly from the source—men—than if I had gone elsewhere.

The other assumption is that the majority of my readers will be women. After working as the *Today* show's men's correspondent, I am familiar with the audience, considering that two thirds of the program's viewers are women. Those viewers watched and listened closely to my reports, commented freely with letters and phone calls, and always came back for more.

Ironically, women have more information to evaluate the Strategic Defense Initiative—Star Wars—than they have to evaluate the men in their lives. Until recent years, although twin beds were separate but equal, not much else was. The sexual apartheid has left women groping for answers, and at a serious disadvantage.

The confusion, consternation, and frustration that many feel from being left in the dark has created tension and misunderstanding. Women have tried to get answers, but they get the runaround instead.

II

I had already established the first men's "beat" in the history of network TV news and launched my syndicated newspaper column for King Features when I met a woman who provided me with a central metaphor that brilliantly captured what this book is all about. She told me that she had a friend named Doug. They had known each other for years, and Doug functioned as a spy, bringing her information from behind the men's locker-room door. He was there when she needed advice about men: "What did he mean when he said . . . ?" "Why does he . . . ?" "Doesn't he understand that . . . ?"

It hit me then that every woman needs a spy to go behind men's lines and into foreign territory that in so many ways could be the landscape of another planet. I hereby volunteer for hazardous duty—but not an impossible mission—to be your spy. Not the sinister cloak-and-dagger variety; more like a user-friendly secret agent.

And it is hazardous duty. There will be good news and bad news to report; you may be tempted to tar and feather the messenger. In the pages ahead I expect you'll learn a lot of things you didn't know about men, and you'll rediscover stuff that you knew, but didn't know that you knew.

III

I've constructed the chapters around the men and the women I've talked to over the years as I traveled around the United States gathering material for my broadcasts, columns, and lectures. I have benefited from the kindness of strangers (and many friends) who shared the intimate details of their lives with me. I've changed names and hometowns, but not the stories. The pleasure and the pain are all there. It's up to you to transform these ingredients into the substance of your own life.

Occasionally, we'll take a break from these case studies and anecdotes for some straight questions and answers. It gives me a chance to pretend I'm Ann Landers.

What's not pretended is my effort to act as an honest broker of information. I have strong opinions and recommendations; I'll express them, as I have often done on *Donahue, Attitudes, Sally Jessy Raphäel,* and in other forums. Ultimately, though, I step back and let my readers make up their own minds.

IV

Every journalist confronts this question—stated with varying degrees of emphasis: Who the hell appointed you? In my case, the answer is, I appointed myself.

When I began my association with NBC, it was as if I had walked into the Pentagon press room and discovered that no reporters had been assigned to cover the army. *Today* was broadcasting segments on sports, medicine, movies, and politics; women's issues had been highlighted for years. But men weren't even an afterthought. As one of the show's platoon of contributing correspondents, I was able to change that.

After all, I've got an important credential for the job of being a men's writer and reporter—I'm a man. I enjoy being one, and I take great pleasure in the differences between men and women. Those differences are the kindling that fires up our sexuality and makes it so exciting when we are together.

Another credential comes to me by way of an accident of birth. My mother was a New York City cop. I like to say that she carried me in her womb and a .38 in her purse. She taught me that it is not a "man's world" at all. The world belongs to anybody who is smart and tough and loving and ready.

My father, also a New York City cop, went on to change careers and become a psychoanalyst. He co-authored the best seller *How to Be Your Own Best Friend.* In so many important ways, that book is the foundation for this one. Men and women can be *best* friends.

V

I'd like to round off my introduction with a visual image even though this is a book, not television—a scene from a busy street corner in lower Manhattan:

They were lost. An attractive couple in a green Toyota. He was behind the wheel, frowning. She was in the passenger seat, smiling and waving a road map at me from the open window. I heard "Holland Tunnel . . . ?" over the traffic noise. And as I described the best route, the woman carefully jotted notes on a scrap of paper. Her husband fiddled with the radio and otherwise pretended that he was not involved in the process of escaping from the maze of streets that had so confused and angered him.

It wasn't difficult to get them pointed in the right direction; the tunnel was only a few blocks away. As they drove off, I wondered how many women had been on similar "joy rides" since Henry Ford gave us the Model T. Most men—and I'm one of them—just can't bring themselves to stop and ask directions. We've probably been avoiding it since that distant ancestor first climbed on the back of a horse.

And I bet that you've done exactly what the woman in the green Toyota did. She persuaded, begged, cajoled, demanded, wheedled, reasoned, and employed every high- and low-pressure sales tool to get the man behind the wheel to stop and ask a few simple questions, such as "Where are we?" and "How do I get out of here?"

Well, I wrote this book for her—for you—and any other woman who knows that taking another wrong turn is not the right way to get where she is going.

All too often women have been treated like the tourists in the old joke about the Yankee farmer and the folks from out of town who needed directions to Bangor: "Bangor? You want to go to Bangor? Try taking a left at the old red barn . . . or maybe it's a right . . ." There's a pause and then the punchline: "Come to think of it, you can't get there from here."

Solid, fulfilling relationships with men? Happiness? Love? Come to think of it, you can get there from here.

CHAPTER ONE

MEN ARE DIFFERENT . . .

Somewhere between the invention of lite beer and lite beef, the ultimate "lite" product made an appearance—lite men.

Less fat, more tender, and tastefully dressed, he was the ideal product for the 1970s. A man for all microwaves. Women chewed on him for a while, but in the end spit him out.

While it lasted, the vogue for lite men did have an effect. The flabby, tough, and tasteless standard of macho excellence began to change. Taunted and tutored by feminists, we started to appreciate two-income households, female orgasms, and quality time with the kids.

There have been a lot of ideas floating around about men; we picked up on some of the best and watered down our worst instincts.

We're not lite. We're not perfect. But we *have* changed.

Women have changed too. I'm probably going to touch off a my-change-is-bigger-than-your-change contest by saying this, but here goes: I've always felt that women overestimate how much they've changed and underestimate how much men have changed. And it's easy to see why. The life-style of women has been radically altered. By comparison, men are still living in the Edwardian Age.

We go to work and come home in the same old way. We re-create and procreate in the same old way.

Women, however, like Dorothy in *The Wizard of Oz*, were swept out of Kansas by a tornado of changing values, economic conditions, and sexual mores.

They can take credit for making some of these changes come about. But many changes occurred because of circumstances beyond their control. Similarly, men have been swept along by the tides and the tornadoes. We've changed because it was easier to change than to fight the change.

But in one key area, where it would be much easier not to budge, to hang on and slug it out, men are making a series of especially difficult changes. Men are giving up power. In going about it, some of us are more graceful than others. The diehards oppose equal pay for equal work (talk about lost causes!). The rest of us are saving our ammunition to snipe at the changes that really go against the grain, and the choice of targets depends on who's pulling the trigger. Fred may blaze away to keep his club from admitting women. Joe can't stand the thought of a woman in the White House. Bruce won't work for a woman.

The guerrilla war against change is being waged by women as well, and men are getting caught in the cross fire because women refuse to take the power that they have every right to claim.

Example: picking up the bill for dinner during a date. When men and women go out today, even some hardcore feminists fall into a time warp, and the spirits of their mothers and grandmothers take control of their bodies as soon as the check comes. Their arms are paralyzed and they just can't manage to reach out for that slip of paper.

Many women are unable to overcome this disability. They still expect the guy to pay.

"He's making more money than I do" doesn't cut it. First of all, that's not necessarily true anymore. Second, if one of your girlfriends calls with a luncheon invitation, I doubt whether there's a comparison of W-2 forms over coffee and dessert to determine who pays.

Example: the reluctance to initiate social and sexual encounters with men. It is a traditional male role that many women pull back from. If he doesn't call, she sits at home. If he doesn't come on, she doesn't get off.

Confronting Change

Men are confused by this off-again-on-again passivity. Hugh, a landscape contractor, had a very short-lived affair with one of his clients. It lived exactly three dates. The first two were the predictable get-acquainted encounters, but the third, with the relationship warming, was full of promise until Hugh showed up at Kit's office to take her to dinner. As they left the building, she asked where they were going to eat, and he said he hadn't made a choice, thinking that they would discuss it as they drove. Kit refused to speak another word for the next twenty blocks. She was furious. Baffled, Hugh figured Kit had been having a bad day. He tried to share some of his "horror" stories about the job, but she obviously wasn't listening. "Okay," he finally asked, "what's wrong?"

"Don't ask me to choose a restaurant. I want you to make those kinds of decisions," Kit said. They ate in a pizza franchise that night, and it was the last time they saw each other.

What turned Hugh off, I suspect, was that, after finally "graduating" to relationships in which he was not expected to dominate at every turn, after getting comfortable with negotiation and compromise, Kit was a reminder of the way things used to be. What was most damaging to Hugh's ego was an implied criticism that he was somehow neglecting his duty as a man.

Courtship patterns change quickly on the surface. Underneath, there is a core of values and beliefs that remains fixed for longer periods, perhaps as long as a lifetime. The conflict creates tension, and to relieve it we—men and women—resort to all kinds of dodges. We avoid commitments. We adopt "liberated" life-styles. We turn celibacy into a philosophy. We find somebody else to blame for the problem.

Penny was organized. Make that o-r-g-a-n-i-z-e-d. She had a genius for staying on top of the details of life. Ben was her exact opposite. He was a study in confusion: The checkbook was never balanced; tax records were a mess; the bills never got paid on time. But as long as they lived together, Penny insisted that Ben keep the household accounts. And it was a source of constant friction. Ben tried, but he was incorrigible. When Penny would reluctantly step in to straighten things out, she would let Ben know that it was a major imposition. There was always a quarrel around the end of the month.

For Penny, that core of beliefs and values which I mentioned earlier included in its many layers the image of a man—probably her father—sitting at the dining-room table paying the mortgage, the utility bills, and the other living expenses of the family. The notion, as comforting as it must have been, was in direct conflict with Penny's principles as a modern woman. She believed in equal sharing of responsibilities, but assigned

the wrong task to Ben, assuming he would change his
ways for her.

The way out of the conflict was to conclude that Ben
was being stubborn and perverse. They eventually drifted
apart. And Ben is still regularly bouncing checks.

Each person has his or her own private status quo.
These are things we would like to see stay exactly the way
they are. Our status quo can either be a comfort or a curse,
by providing a solid anchor on one hand, or repressing us
with a narrow, suffocating choice of options on the other
(most often it is a little of both). Unfortunately, we have a
hard time figuring out which is which. When men and
women pair off, there is confusion and consternation as we
try to reconcile two sets of status quo. We fall back on an attitude that John F. Kennedy saw demonstrated during a
round of international-trade talks in the early 1960s: "What's
mine is mine, and what's yours is negotiable," he quipped.

I think that explains why trench warfare set in after the
early feminist victories. There's been hardly any move-
ment in recent years. Once the major issues were confronted, we got tangled in the barbed wire of the status
quo. And ever since, steady criticism of men seems to be
coming from the "what's yours is negotiable" side of the
free-fire zone.

A Matter of Principle

Ann is a very attractive, intelligent woman. She hadn't
been out on a date in a long time, but met a guy and the
chemistry was right. They had dinner, a few drinks afterward, and ended up in bed.

The next day, I got a call from her. She told me that

he was a great guy and that she really liked him. Everything was perfect—except . . . And while I hear a lot of "excepts," this one did catch me off guard. "I feel like I am betraying my feminist principles," she said. "The truth of the matter is that I really like having a penis inside me during sex."

"That's a betrayal of feminist principles?" I asked.

"Yes, we're not supposed to be so dependent on men."

Huh?

Sometimes I take my time pondering and weighing a proper response, and in this case I gave it a full two tenths of a second: "Why not? We're dependent on each other. It's one of the wonderful things about men and women."

Celebrating the Differences

We've lived with the myth, over the last twenty-five years, that men and women are the same. *Myth* is a strong word, and I have to say that I'm not using it to knock the basic principles of feminism, which have had a profound and beneficial impact on all of us. But I've never been comfortable with the notion that gender is purely a matter of who has what organs and body parts. I asked a group of male feminists to explain the difference between men and women—and they couldn't tell me. I asked Phil Donahue, a guy who has spent hours of television time criticizing and analyzing men, to define the term *masculine*—and he couldn't do it.

There is a difference. Why deny it? We should celebrate our differences. And to be sure, there are similarities: We all have spleens, hearts, lungs—things like that. Even on the emotional side, I believe the one thing that men and women have in common is the need to love and be loved.

I'd say we share that with every single human being on earth.

Even so, we are not the same. We see the world from different angles, different viewpoints, different languages. A comedian friend of mine says that he looks at the world "funny." When I asked him what he meant by that, he explained that people can look at a set of objects in a room—a TV set, a desk, a lamp—and the reality is the same, but it is the way each individual looks at them that makes them different. Celebrate the differences.

It's gotten to the point where men have become the outcasts of society. Tune in on a nearby conversation at a restaurant or bar, and you'll probably hear: "This person I'm going out with." Why can't they say "This man . . . ?" "This man I'm going out with." There seems to be a problem with forming the word—*m . . . m . . . man*. It is a three-letter word, an okay word: *m-a-n*.

If we keep bashing men over the head, they are going to become alienated and uncommunicative—exactly what women claim they don't like in men. Shere Hite, in her book on male sexuality, has a subchapter on men who are still hostile toward women's liberation. She quotes a man as saying that he believes in equal rights and equal opportunity for men and women, but thinks women should be feminine and should help men to feel manly. I read the comment several times and still couldn't understand what it was doing on a page that was supposed to be dealing with male hostility toward women's liberation. How is that statement hostile to women's liberation and feminist goals? That attitude is not harming anyone; it helps, in a practical, common-sense way, by directing attention to the differences that are the foundation of our distinct individuality and sexuality. Let's not try to remake ourselves into Ken and Barbie dolls with interchangeable parts.

CHAPTER TWO

THE BASIC MAN

This probably won't strike you as a terrible surprise, but I might as well come right out and say what has to be said: Guys can be completely oblivious to something that has a profound effect on women. Before I drown in a wave of sarcastic comments—"No kidding, Bob . . . I didn't know that"—let me quickly add the key ingredient: We're not being deliberately callous, or "playing dumb" to get a rise out of you. These behavior patterns, patterns that often perplex and frustrate women, are influenced by our gender.

I'm not suggesting that "My chromosomes made me do it" is the all-purpose defense for forgetting things like wedding anniversaries and birthdays. The point is—men are not women.

Men are much simpler than women. I didn't say "simple," or "simpletons." Simply simpler. We are different, and there's more to those differences than just the placement and configuration of our reproductive organs.

But by coming right out and saying that men are simpler than women, I am running the risk of being misinterpreted. It is easy to get in trouble with the connotation of a word. *Simple* can be read as "inferior" or "defective," and that's not what I mean at all. I also don't mean that this simplicity is a badge of honor, as though simple were good, complexity bad.

Let's forget the value judgments and take a look at a classic example of one of the basic differences between *a* man and *a* woman. The woman is Debbie. She has a special technique for communicating with her husband, Richard. When they are driving on the freeway—Debbie and Richard live in California, so they spend more time in the car than in bed—she pops a Billy Joel tape into the cassette machine and turns up the volume.

Debbie reserves Billy Joel for her angry moments. Rather than confront Richard with her anger, she lets the lyrics of the entertainer's songs speak on her behalf.

Billy Joel says it all, and he says it in stereo.

The problem is that Richard has never been clued into the significance of Billy Joel's message. He is listening to music; Debbie's anger, the portents of trouble, are lost in the morning smog that hangs over Los Angeles.

When Debbie told me about her Billy Joel technique, and Richard's irritating habit of not paying any attention, I congratulated her for showing such subtlety. And I was only being slightly sarcastic. It is often difficult to express and direct our anger toward someone we love. Wouldn't it be marvelous to find a way to say the painful things that must be said without having to do it face-to-face?

The Billy Joel tape was a good idea, but it didn't work.

Debbie and I went for a drive so that I could listen to the tape. I played it through a couple of times and said, "Debbie, why are you doing this? Do you think that he's that subtle? The man is wheeling a car down a freeway at eighty miles an hour, and you're asking for a close textual analysis of a Billy Joel song. Who's going to get this? You explained it to me, and I still don't get it. What makes you think Richard is going to get it? Tell him!"

What seemed perfectly clear to Debbie was perfectly unclear to Richard. He wasn't being insensitive or indifferent. Richard was just being a man. Women hint; they read each other loud and clear. But men need it spelled out.

The Old Magazine Trick

Jill had a good thing going with Wayne. They were living together, and the relationship was clearly headed toward marriage. But she wanted to tell him that she wasn't absolutely positive she could be monogamous for the rest of her life. It was possible, but Jill just wasn't sure, and she wanted to be completely honest about her doubts. Naturally, the subject was sensitive. You don't say, "Oh, by the way, I think I may feel like cheating on you from time to time."

What she did was a variation on Debbie's Billy Joel number. Those tests that are forever showing up in the women's magazines—"How Sexy Are You?"; "Rate Your Jealousy Quotient"; and so on—seemed like the perfect way to let Wayne know what was on her mind. She went through one that was supposed to measure a person's capacity for playing around on the side, and she checked off all the boxes that indicated that being faithful was simply not in the cards. Jill left the incriminating evidence on her boyfriend's pillow and waited.

Wayne, like most guys, looked at it and said, "Honey, you left your magazine over here. Do you want it, or should I toss it?"

So much for subtlety!

In the end, Jill realized that she had to take the plunge and tell him directly. It worked out perfectly. Jill didn't realize it, but he was having the same fears. Wayne was glad that she had brought it up and said, "I'm not so sure I can be monogamous either. I'll try my best, but I don't know what's going to happen down the road." They ended up married, and the last I heard they were quite happy together. Maybe they are and maybe they aren't monogamous. But that initial investment in honesty and directness worked to bring them together.

Women have a knack for sending and receiving signals. Most men aren't built that way. Why? One theory is that the traditional male role of defending the family conditioned us to take events at face value. A stranger at the gate was an enemy to be fought and defeated. He who hesitated was lost. The need to take immediate action overwhelmed the instinct to analyze the situation.

Behind the wheel, Richard is confronting dozens of strangers and enemies every second. He is not tuned in to signals from Debbie transmitted via Billy Joel songs. To Wayne, a magazine is a magazine, not a fortune cookie that will reveal Jill's misgivings about monogamy.

Both Jill and Debbie asked me for advice, and this is what I told them: If you hint and signal and a man picks up on the message more than three times out of ten, head for Las Vegas because you're one lucky lady.

Hinting may pay off; it's probably worth a try. But recognize from the outset that the odds are not in your favor.

If you speak up and tell a man what's on your mind —"Listen, we have a problem and here's why"—there may be a discussion, even a heated argument, but not the confusion and consternation that comes from making assumptions that turn out to be way off base. Maybe he didn't get the hint. Maybe the message went right over his head. Review your past assumptions about other men, and ask whether they have proven out in the end. If the track record isn't very impressive, it's time to make one last assumption—assume that you're going to be wrong.

There's never an easy way to handle painful subjects. However, I think it might be made easier, less traumatic, by taking a series of small steps toward a resolution rather than seeking a quick fix. I double-checked with psychologist Neal Newman to make sure that I'm not contradicting myself by advocating directness on one hand, and what may seem like indirection on the other.

"Taking small steps toward goals is not being indirect," Dr. Newman said. "It's just moving toward what you want in bite-size chunks. Going one step at a time increases the chances that your partner can take in and respond positively to your requests." He points out that it's not unusual for individuals to have a long list of grievances. "Let's say five things are bothering you. Instead of trying to resolve all five at one sitting, spoon them out . . . do one at a time. This involves determining your priorities. You don't want to overwhelm your partner with demands. If he is feeling smothered, burdened, controlled, or taken advantage of by you, he probably will not respond to your needs in the way you would like best."

Dr. Newman told me that "couples must have reasonable goals and expectations of their partner. This involves an appraisal of not only your needs but also of your partner's own needs and his capacity for meeting your needs. To expect that your partner must cater to your every whim is to invite disappointment."

Dr. Newman believes "it is important to assert your

wants and your rights to your wants. However, it is up to you to pick what is worth fighting for. Everything is not worthy of a fight."

He adds, "It is also useful to assume that your partner is not your enemy. Since you are allies, it is sensible to expect that it will be possible to work *with* him to attain your goals."

Problems don't sprout overnight like mushrooms. It's unrealistic to expect that a few minutes of blunt talk will mend a damaged relationship. It's often best to move slowly. Give him a chance to focus on the issue and your position. Introspection, analysis, and self-knowledge need time and a temperate atmosphere in order to develop.

When threatened, men tend to go on the attack. After all, from the very first day of playing kickball in elementary school to varsity football in college, we've been told over and over again that the best defense is a good offense.

By approaching the rough spots in your relationship as though you were playing a long game of chess, one that's being carried out over several days or weeks, it's possible to drain away much of the bitterness that might otherwise explode.

The key to success is to keep everything up front. Subtlety is fine for a French film, but terrible for American men. Be direct.

When in Doubt, Ask

Allison is a lawyer in Chicago, but she must have spent too much time with Blackstone and other legal texts, and not enough studying philosophy with Professor Flip Wilson. The comedian's famous line "What you see is what you get" should be carved into granite. When the man Allison was living with advised her to take a year off from her high-pressure job, she read the suggestion as a signal that he was ready for her to have a child. Allison was listening to the ticking of her biological clock and looking for signals from David that he was not sending in the first place. He was concerned about career burnout, not babies. David wanted Allison to take a break. The misunderstanding eventually wrecked their relationship.

I do think Allison would have been better off if she had raised the subject of children directly. Even so, David was hiding from reality. If he had opened his ears, he too would have heard the biological clock. You don't have to be an obstetrician to know how to tell time. Allison was approaching her mid-thirties, but David was the one who did not want to face up to the facts of life. He wasn't ready to be a father, or even to confront the possibility, and the easy thing to do was to pretend that Allison was just one of the "guys" getting stressed out on a demanding job.

Like Allison, many women see live-in relationships as a prelude to marriage. Often, they are. Yet plenty of men are out there right now in live-in arrangements, and the idea of marriage has never entered their heads. Perhaps they are fighting off the responsibilities of the adult world. Or maybe they are too preoccupied with the demands of a new career to focus on the ultimate bottom line of a relationship that began with the fine, freewheeling sexuality of two young people in a hurry to learn what life was all about.

Whatever the reason, Allison and David were not good at communicating with each other. The confusion started with "Hey, why don't you move into my place?" Allison thought the words meant love, commitment, marriage, children. David saw them as good sex, good company, good times.

As it turned out, David was right. The sex was terrific; they were friends and had a lot of fun.

And David was wrong. He was wrong for Allison. If I could, I would turn back the clocks, the one that measures real time and the one that keeps track of biological time, so that she could ask the man she loved a few important —direct—questions.

Watching What He Does, Not What He Says

It's not bad enough that we complicate life for women by being simple, but men add to the confusion by speaking a different language. It's another reason why men and women have such difficulty communicating with each other. Having set myself up as the Berlitz of men—actually, my franchise is called Boylitz—I am often asked by women to translate. It's not an easy job. With a foreign language you can fall back on the dictionary and a book of grammar. But every man works with a different built-in thesaurus, scrambling the words and improvising the meanings as he goes.

For the fun of it, I've worked up a rough guide that pairs the sound of what men say with the sense of what they mean. The results are unscientific, and mostly tongue-in-cheek, though I think you'll find it useful to spend a few moments considering the very real gulf that can exist between the message and its meaning.

Bob's Sex Lex

When he says, "Sure, I like kids," he means: "I like kids, but I'm not ready to settle down and have four of them before I buy my first Porsche."

When he says, "I could see myself married someday," he means: "I'm not just another playboy, but for now, let's play."

When he says, "I lived with a woman once, but it didn't work out," he means: "I'm willing to make commitments, but nothing is ever set in concrete."

When he says, "Tell me about your ex-boyfriends," he means: "Tell me about the losers and creeps."

When he says, "What's your favorite color?" he means: "Maybe I can get my money back if she doesn't like pink."

When he says, "Did you see the _____s play last night?" he means: "If she's a _____s fan, I've found the perfect woman."

When he says, "My shower is broken. Can I come over and use yours?" he means: "If you'll wash my back, I'll wash yours."

When he says, "I'm really into my job," he means: "My career comes first."

When he says, "My wife and I are separated," he means: "My wife is out on the West Coast and I'm here in Cleveland."

When he says, "My wife and I are separated," he means: "My wife and I are separated."

When he says, "Let's just be friends," he means: "There are other women in my life."

When he says, "Let's just have some fun and see where we end up," he means: "I like you but it's too early to make any commitments."

When he says, "We could go back to my place, but it's a little messy," he means: "I'm a slob."

When he says, "Would you mind going to [Sunday] brunch without me? I've got a lot of paperwork to do," he means: "There is no way I'm going to miss that game."

When he says, "Wanna drive?" he means: "I'm too drunk [stoned, ill, tired, etc.] to drive."

When he says, "You look stressed out. Roll over and I'll rub your back," he means: "Let's make love."

When he says, "I wonder what Koppel is doing on *Nightline* tonight," he means: "Not tonight."

When he says, "Let's talk about it some other time," he means: "The subject is closed."

This lexicon is a good starting point. Add your own translations, or, better still, go behind a man's lines and confront his actions. There, face-to-face with what he is doing, rather than floating in the bubble of what he is saying, you will find his meaning. Men speak through their actions. They're not good at verbalizing.

The Language Barrier Stops Traffic

Even guys who are paid for their communications skills have trouble delivering a basic message. Ian was a top Washington journalist, a member of the White House press corps, when I got to know him. It's a job that has destroyed more than one man's family life thanks to the long hours and days on the road. A weekend off can be a rarity. Despite all that, Ian was able to launch a successful long-term relationship with Jessica because she realized one Sunday when he arrived at her apartment with *The New York Times* tucked under his arm that he was telling her something very important: He wanted to share one of his most precious commodities—a free, no-hassle, no-ringing-phones, no-hysterical-editors Sunday—and he wanted to share it with her.

Jessica, fortunately, did not need words (and it was a lucky thing because Ian would have suffered Chinese water torture and still kept quiet about his real feelings). The action was enough to persuade her that Ian was serious.

It is too bad that men are not more articulate about their emotions. Talking things out is an excellent way to relieve anxiety and to clarify an uncertain situation. Silence can often mask a refusal to face up to reality—pretend, like the ostrich, that it's not there and it will go away. A woman's ability to discuss sensitive subjects, while at times painful to her, is a way to deal with reality. But men are still in the dark and silent ages. In some ways, it's comparable to a different culture. No sophisticated traveler would touch down in La Paz and demand that Bolivians speak English and give up their local customs. "Be civilized!! I can't understand a word you're saying. What's this nap time in the middle of the day all about? And we eat dinner at six o'clock back in Akron. You should, too."

Bolivians aren't about to change. They speak Spanish; it fits their needs and history; their life-style has evolved over centuries. The same thing goes for men. It would

make life a lot easier for women if we spoke your language
and approached life with your frame of references, but we
don't.

Subtlety is the Enemy of Clarity

Let's take a quick backward glance at the three examples
I cited in this chapter: Allison was mistranslating and
Debbie got into trouble because she was using complex
sign language; they both were overlooking the actions
that were the real language. Jessica, the one who got
home delivery of the *Times*, via Ian, didn't make the same
mistake.

Women can get over the language barrier most effectively by telling men what it is they want out of a relationship. Make your needs known. As I said earlier,
hinting doesn't work.

I know it's frustrating. You probably want to bang your
head against the wall and say, "What's wrong with this
guy? Can't he take a hint?" The answer is—no, he can't.
To communicate with a man—and, of course, I'm talking
about a level of communication that can sustain a fulfilling relationship—both of you must speak a common
language.

Now, there is a contradiction in my position that you've
probably already noticed. I'm telling women that they
should stop using their native tongue. The Bolivian analogy cuts both ways. Like Spanish and those local customs
I mentioned, the language that women speak fits their
needs and experience.

So we have an impasse. We're stuck.

Or are we? Given the extraordinary pace of change in
the last one hundred years, both languages—his and

hers—are as dead as Latin. The race is on to reinvent a language that works for men and women.

Don't ask me why, but I have a gut feeling that women will get there first.

And I'll give you a head start right here: You may think he understands those artful, subtle gestures, but he probably doesn't. And once you've made your position clear, start watching his actions.

CHAPTER THREE

THE OPEN MAN

Men would be in big trouble without Western Union. We need somebody to deliver our messages—a dirty job, and one that men have never learned to handle.

As a result, this question is asked again and again: "Why can't he open up and tell me what he's feeling?"

In many cases, he does tell you what he is feeling. Just as women send subtle signals, men use a primitive telegraph system—something on the order of a couple of orange juice cans and string. We're task and job oriented, so the code takes the form of action.

Warren Farrell, who wrote *Why Men Are the Way They Are*, points out that a coal miner who works a double shift under grueling and hazardous conditions just so that his children can go to college and escape from a life like their father's is expressing his love for the family even though he is incapable of saying the words—"I love you so much." Action is his language.

I've heard women object to Warren's coal miner as an example of the way men express their emotions. They thought I was suggesting that men are better, when I was actually pointing out *differences* between men and women. The skeptics figured that there was a covert message in

Warren's observation—men act and women only talk. But I don't read it that way, because you'd have to search long and hard to find a man—he'd be one in a million—who would agree with the proposition that women are "all talk." The old us-versus-them battle is a dead-end street. It's important to look to a man's actions (good or bad); you may wait forever if you are waiting for words.

The coal miner is not better than his wife, just different. His wife has made her share of sacrifices—but I was talking about men, and they are the subject of this book. In the last twenty-five years, millions of words have been written about women, and I will leave that field of study to others.

I'm not interested in sending women or men off to stand in the corner of the room until they learn how to behave themselves like ladies and gentlemen; I'm not Emily Post. And I'm not having any part of an us-versus-them grudge match.

There's no hidden meaning to what I'm saying. Men are different. D-I-F-F-E-R-E-N-T.

Easy Does It (Almost) Every Time

Figuring out what a man wants from a relationship and marriage takes detective work. He may tell you, but chances are you will have to fit together the pieces of a jigsaw puzzle. It's necessary to become an investigative reporter.

To do this successfully, fight the temptation to reject the obvious. Why look for the most convoluted explanations for things and overlook what's staring you in the face? Often, there is less there than meets the eye.

If all the signs point to the conclusion that a guy only wants you to take care of him, make a nice home, feed him his meals, and have regular sex with him—believe it. That's what he wants. Don't ask him to open up and reveal his "real" emotional requirements; he already has.

Do men operate on such a primitive level? You *know* some of them do. Am I saying that all men see women in those crude terms? No. There is much more to the majority of relationships between men and women than sex, a full stomach, and good housekeeping.

By offering such a stark example, I'm trying to persuade you to think like a minimalist. Perhaps the man in your life is secretly complex. He may be using the techniques of an abstract painter to conceal the intricate mechanism of his universe behind straight lines and flat planes. Men are wary about exposing their vulnerabilities, and once the bonds of trust are established between the two of you, the complexity may emerge. But if the man is, in fact, all straight lines and flat planes, the heavy load of extra ornamentation that you're seeing may ruin an important relationship.

We all have plenty of gadgets and appliances around our homes, and whenever one of mine refuses to work right I always start with the easiest solution to the problem. I check to see if the thing is plugged in, switched on, or needs a new bulb. Jumping to the wrong conclusion, guessing that a fuse is blown, the transistors shot, or the wiring crossed can mean hours of frustration and expense. Maybe it will help to think of men as another version of the electric toaster, although I doubt whether banks will ever give one out with each new account. In sorting through the potential answers to the question "What does he want?"—start with the basics.

Mutual ego support, love and a secure environment, sex. These are not impossible dreams for two people to share and achieve. Less really is more—because it is obtainable, workable, nourishing. Every great cathedral stands on a basic foundation . . . or, every working toaster is connected with a simple plug.

Looking Good and Good-looking

The tendency to overlook the stark reality of the basic man starts early in life. The first dress that's purchased in order to grab the attention of a "special" boy is where it begins. Then come fancy haircuts, cosmetics, and diets. In the end, probably 90 percent of all the effort failed to register.

Men are oblivious to much of what women do to interest and attract them. I said "much," and this is where it's easy to lose track of what is and isn't getting through.

Let me set the scene: an elegant restaurant in a major East Coast city; four men in their twenties and thirties are enjoying dinner; there are lots of laughs and excellent conversation around the table. A good-looking couple enters the main dining room. The woman is wearing a see-through blouse, without a bra.

What a surprise! The guys notice. They aren't looking at her eye shadow, or noting that the gold bracelet and earrings match. They are admiring—all conversation on hold—her breasts.

As the couple moves across the room, it becomes perfectly obvious that they are being watched by an appreciative audience. When she gets into range, the woman turns to the nearest man at the table and snaps, "What do you think you're staring at?" Under the circumstances, it's a question that rates with Groucho's "Who's buried in Grant's tomb?"

What did she think they were looking at? What was

the point of wearing the revealing blouse in the first place? Those four men weren't blind.

But again, they didn't notice the expensive haircut and the manicure. It wasn't a matter of being rude, or immature, or sex-crazed. When it comes to women, a man's optic nerves run directly to his crotch.

The news shouldn't be much of a shock, but the facts of life get rearranged by those who like to sell a new line of fall fashions, designer cosmetics, or high-speed liposuctions.

Men are "supposed" to be turned on by a particular shade of lipstick. Men are "supposed" to be turned on by little button noses. Men are "supposed" to be turned on by skinny women. Says who? Cosmetic czars? Plastic surgeons? Millionaire diet doctors?

The message that gets lost in the chorus of special-interest pleading is the most important one of all: Men like women—in all their diversity.

A Cosmetic-Counter Attack

Trouble sets in when the apples and oranges get jumbled together. What's fashionable or appeals to women goes into the bin marked Granny Smith, Delicious, or McIntosh. What impacts on men belongs with the Sevilles and navels.

I participated in a panel discussion with a woman who made a real fruit salad by arguing that cosmetics are part of a plot by men to tyrannize women. The audience, 99 percent female, nearly hooted her off the stage.

In a roundabout way she was confirming my point of view. If a woman spends hundreds of dollars and hours on makeup to attract men, she is being tyrannized—not by men, but by expectations that can never be fulfilled. It's the tyranny of hope over experience. The fruit-salad lady goes several steps beyond by contending that men are to blame, when they, in fact, couldn't care less. (And many men have told me that they believe women wear too much makeup.)

I've interviewed dozens of men who said that some of their most satisfying relationships had been with women who weren't conventionally beautiful or well dressed. But they were sexy and fun to be around.

Those women are onto something crucial. They've zeroed in on the essential ingredients of a successful relationship with a man. They've freed themselves from the tyranny of the "supposed to's."

Skin and Bones

There is a machine at my health club that is an absolute killer. It's designed to tighten up the abdominal muscles. Every day for two weeks running my friend Robin was on that thing, and she was suffering. Why? She was going to the Caribbean on vacation and she had to take an extra inch off her waist. She looked great, but that inch became an obsession.

Men are largely immune to fashions and trends and are less susceptible to fat phobia, which sends women off on torturous diet routines that are questionable at best, actually dangerous to their health at worst. Keeping a few pounds off is fine, but anorexia is not sexy.

The media have sold women a bill of goods. There are a lot of men out there who like women with some fat on them—not pleasingly plump, but fat.

Obviously, you have to decide what's best for your own

health. There are risks in being overweight; I'm not rec-
ommending obesity. But sanity dictates some retreat from
the Madison Avenue image of women.

I've seen an audience applaud when a woman stood
up and announced that she had lost ninety-five pounds.
It was as if she had performed a morally courageous act.
The suggestion seems to be that fat is inferior, that if you're
not skinny you're a second-class citizen.

If a svelte waistline is so important, why do the legal
bordellos in Nevada always feature at least one, and usually more, Rubenesque woman? That old-fashioned look
is definitely out, and has been for decades, yet those who
practice the world's oldest profession don't seem to care.

Opening Your Ears

Lou's country house is the place to be on rainy August
days. He has a fabulous library, and his friends love to
stop by unannounced to ransack the paperback fiction for
weekend reading material. One summer, though, Charles,
one of Lou's best buddies, found that on nearly every visit
the place was swarming with kids.

Charles kept his mouth shut for a while—the book
mooch should never look the book horse in the mouth—
but finally he couldn't help himself.

"What's with all the midgets?" Charles asked after
tracking Lou to the garage where he was replacing the
pads on the brakes of his vintage Studebaker, a job he
does only when he is in a bad mood.

"Don't ask," he said.

"Too late; I just did."

Lou tapped the naked brake drum with the handle of
a screwdriver. "Those aren't midgets," he said. "Unfor-

tunately. If they were we could all be doing some serious beer drinking." He paused to pump the jack handle a couple of times. "Those short people out there are members of Cassie's brainwashing crew. Since the Fourth of July she has had me on the permanent-press cycle. By Labor Day I am supposed to be in the mood for a little parenting."

Charles pointed out to Lou that he was already a parent—twice.

"I am? Must have slipped my mind," he replied sarcastically.

Charles helped out by reminding him of the names of his children, both in their twenties. He suggested that the information be passed along to Cassie, his girlfriend. At the time, Lou had been divorced for nearly ten years.

"I have a hunch she knows already," Lou said.

Lou lost interest in the brake pads and started tinkering with the front license-plate holder. "And she also knows that I have no interest whatsoever in an encore. One brood of children is enough," he said. Charles asked him if he had told Cassie his views on the subject. "We discussed it once for three solid days, right before she moved in. I remember it so clearly I can quote myself. 'I don't have any problem with marriage; I don't have any problem with kids . . . as long as they're somebody else's kids.' "

"What did she say?"

"It depended on the day," Lou said. "On the first day, she teased me about being insecure and selfish. On the second day, she said she wasn't in any hurry to have kids. And on the third day, it was, 'Okay, I understand—no kids.' "

"It sounds like something I would say," Charles interjected. "Not very original, but to the point."

Lou was getting irritated by the conversation, and so Charles broke it off and they went back into the house. Charles hung around for a few minutes, watching the tide of children ebb and flow across the place. There were five of them, but it seemed like fifty. Cassie had volunteered to baby-sit for her friends, and Charles wondered if Lou was wrong about the brainwashing. Maybe she was just venting her frustrated maternal instincts. On the way out Charles urged Lou to ask Cassie directly whether she was trying to "sell" him on the idea of having children.

A couple of weeks later Charles saw the Studebaker in the parking lot of the auto-parts store and waited for Lou to come out. "Another brake-pad job?" he inquired of his friend.

"As a matter of fact, you're right. Going to the beach would only spoil my bad mood." Cassie had gone back to the city after their discussion about the kids.

"So much for my great advice," Charles said.

"No, it was solid. I think we'll get back together, and when we do it will be on an honest basis. There won't be any doubt from now on about kids. I just won't tackle that obstacle course again. . . . One lap is enough. Cassie knew that before, but I guess she forgot and needed to be reminded."

Turn back to Chapter Two for a quick refresher course (it's too bad Cassie couldn't have done that). I told you that being direct with a man is essential. But it is a waste of time if your "transmitter" is only sending and not receiving. Switch on the receive mode and listen, listen hard. It is a dangerous gamble to assume that he doesn't mean what he says (and he might not), or that he can be persuaded around to your viewpoint—there's just too much grief waiting out there to make it worth taking a chance. Those who read between the lines run the risk of reading—misreading—the reflection of their own dreams and ignoring the plain and, possibly, painful truth.

The Gypsy Curse

In planning this book, I had discussions with a few women who said, "No, no . . . women don't want to hear that!" They weren't arguing with the substance of my views— that's okay—they were practicing a form of censorship that starts with the notion that we should hear only the things that we want to hear.

When men do open up and tell women how they feel—"Right, you asked for it, and here goes"—some women often get something other than what they bargained for, and they invalidate the guts, the very core, of what they're hearing.

It could be the old gypsy curse: Beware of what you wish for; it may come true. Sometimes a woman will urge a man to open up with his feelings, and when he does, suddenly she will say, in so many words, "Hold the sensitive Alan Alda and get me back to John Wayne!" Be careful, a man may express feelings that you don't want to hear.

Taking a Vow of Silence

Getting a man to talk about what's really eating at him won't be easy. Read his body language; his eyes, in particular, are revealing if he is depressed or bewildered. Drastic changes in behavior patterns—a sound sleeper who turns into a night owl; a reader who doesn't read; a jogger who skips his daily workouts—can indicate inner turmoil.

All of us call for help when we are in trouble. The SOS may be very faint and difficult to understand, but it's there. When you respond, it could seem to him like a rescue ship appearing on the horizon.

If he comes aboard and opens up, you've got to guarantee that whatever he says to you will be held in the strictest confidence. This is very important. So important that I want to circle slowly around the subject and close in on it without stumbling over stereotypes that will make me sound as though I'm saying women can't be trusted with a man's secrets.

The first circle: Men admire and envy women for their friendships with other women. They can talk about their deepest problems, hopes, and fears on a woman-to-woman basis. It is a source of great strength. For us, achieving the same level of verbal intimacy with another man takes enormous effort, courage, and luck.

The second circle: We are dealing with primitive instincts, a self-defense mechanism that cannot easily be switched off for even the best of reasons. To put it simply, men are afraid to lower the drawbridge and open the gate.

Women don't have the same hang-up, and from a distance, men see the advantages of being able to talk things out, but we can't seem to get over the fear that the risks of vulnerability and exposure are too great. Other men are rarely allowed to cross the moat and enter the fortress.

Men will take the risk with a woman, however, if they know their confidences will go no further. They expect women to adopt a male standard and withdraw from the exchange of intimacies that is central to female friendships.

Even the slightest hint that a third party is privy to his secrets will prompt a man to slam shut the gate and never open it again.

The third circle: I am not saying that women can't keep secrets, that they're chatterboxes and blabbermouths. But this is an unvarnished report about men—their impressions and misimpressions—and I can't duck this problem by pretending that it isn't there. A comment, one of many that I picked up while looking for a way to solve it, or at least confront it, helps sharpen the focus: "I'm astonished when I come home in the evening and my wife tells me about the conversation that day with some mothers in the neighborhood. They've talked about things that are eating at them; about their husbands, their children, their financial worries. They air problems that I'd never air with my male friends in a million years."

Get the picture? What you see is a male phobia in action, a phobia that can cripple a life-support system that depends on the ability of two people to communicate about the things that matter to them both.

Phobia is a strong word, but it captures what Barry was feeling when he began to suspect that his girlfriend was talking to others about their relationship. Barry was a member of a camera crew that I was working with on a series of men's stories. He told me that a producer had approached him to say how sorry he was to hear that Barry and Jeanie were having trouble. It came as a shock, because Barry thought his relationship with Jeanie was doing fine. The producer wouldn't say where he had heard the news, and Barry spent days thinking about it. He finally remembered that Jeanie and the producer's assistant went to the same aerobics class.

The idea that one of his colleagues at the network knew about the details of his private life infuriated Barry. He confronted Jeanie; she said that there had been a brief conversation at dance class but that she had spoken to Sally only because she thought the producer's assistant might know if there was something going wrong for Barry at work. The scene wasn't particularly bitter; the couple didn't argue, but the relationship was history in a couple of months. And there are still professional repercussions; Barry steers clear of that producer whenever he can.

Squaring the circles: Yes, I think *phobia* may be the right word. The gate was slammed shut even though Jeanie was looking for answers to an important question. She wanted to know why Barry was moody and depressed and talking about getting out of the TV business. Her motives were pure. But even if Jeanie had been out to zing Barry by using what he had told her as a weapon, the gate would have been slammed shut just as hard and just as fast.

Enough circling. Some men also talk too much; they're insecure and brag about their sexual exploits, although less and less as they get older and wiser. But no matter whether we're talking about men or women, it has been said that information is power, and that's true in politics, business, and love. The way we use information—casually or carefully, by accident or by design—determines if it is to be the power of destruction or of creation.

Sacrificing Life-style for Love-style

Barry opened up to Jeanie for all the right reasons. He needed love and support and a chance to sort out what was happening inside. The process of self-examination is never easy. Having a friend nearby—a friend and a lover—can help ease the pain and uncertainty.

Our best friends, our most intimate friends, bear a

heavy burden. From them, we expect honesty. I'm not talking about the brutal honesty of a physician informing a patient that he has cancer, or a psychotherapist's clinical description of a crippling neurosis. We can all pay stiff professional fees for those kinds of cold facts.

I'm talking about the honesty that grows out of the unique perspective and emotional context that forms around a relationship between a man and a woman. We get to know each other for better and worse. It is knowledge that gives honesty a cutting edge.

In times of crisis, men are their own severest critics. We don't like to admit that we've lost control of a difficult situation, and when it is time to face up to reality, a man can unleash the anger back onto himself. What he needs at that moment is a full measure of that essential, elemental honesty that only you possess.

You see him as no one else does. You know who he is and what he can do. A man depends on that to counteract the punishment he is inflicting on himself. You are his emotional safety net.

How to Criticize a Man

Don't.

Is that the sound of gnashing teeth? Okay, I'll modify the advice. Don't criticize unless you are ready for an argument. Men are not good at taking criticism. The adrenaline starts to flow and the competitive instinct kicks in.

It's not an endearing characteristic, but I promised to tell you what makes men tick, and I wouldn't be doing the job if I edited out the parts that make us seem like spoiled brats.

I'm a perfect example. Criticism drives me up the wall.

But I've come to recognize that "no fault" indirect criticism is more palatable to me and to most other men.

For one thing, indirect criticism doesn't challenge assumptions I've made about who I am and what I stand for. I see myself as reliable, helpful, loving, etc. Whenever this image comes into conflict with reality—perhaps I have failed to fulfill a obligation on time—the mirror cracks. What happens next depends on how good I am at resolving internal contradictions (not the strongest suit of most men).

Being competitive and aggressive, and keeping the faith with all of our square-jawed, steely-eyed role models of yesteryear, we deny that there's been a shortcoming— the reliable, helpful, loving self-image is still intact. We bicker, we quarrel, we fight to protect the icon that we have created.

Another tactic is to put an end to the problem by simply apologizing. Either I don't mean a word of it, or—and this is the darker side of self-image—I see myself as a rotten, unreliable person; my rotten, unreliable behavior and your criticism confirm the negative self-image.

There is no way out of the dilemma, unfortunately. Bottling up your anger to protect his self-image isn't the answer. Take a moment to ask yourself what you hope to accomplish with the criticism. If you are satisfied with the answer, say what has to be said.

Criticizing him behind his back to a relative or one of his friends is one way to avoid an immediate confrontation, but it is only postponing the inevitable blowup. Hearing from a buddy that "your wife thinks you spend too much time tinkering with the car, and not enough with her— Hah! Hah! Hah!" is likely to work like gasoline thrown on an open fire.

Humor and gentle teasing are effective ways to deliver the message. I know one woman who posts a QUARANTINE sign on the door of her husband's study when it's time for him to do some house cleaning. He's a pack rat when it comes to newspaper clippings and magazine articles, and his wife practically breaks out the champagne when he throws anything away. Her exaggerated reaction lets him know that she is not in love with the mess.

A helpful way to develop a light touch as a critic is to listen to how men—I'm thinking of friends—criticize each other. First of all, it doesn't happen very often. There is an element of live and let live. When it does happen, the moment has been carefully chosen, and it usually follows a mellow or upbeat occasion. Once the subject is raised, the discussion tends to be short, unemotional, and to the point. Most of the man-to-man sessions I've been involved in end with the guy who is doing the criticizing giving his friend a face-saving way out: "Well, you must have been drunk . . ." "You were pretty mad . . ." "I'd probably do the same thing myself . . ."

Some people are injustice collectors. They have a long list of complaints ready to go. They come in over the target like an old B-26 with the bomb-bay doors wide open. Helen was an injustice collector, and her relationships with men, one right after the other, ended with incredible firestorms of criticism and anger. She told me that she was trying to be reasonable, and therefore would wait to see if a guy "mended his ways." When he didn't, it was bombs away! I urged her to try telling B.J., her latest boyfriend, what was on her mind when it was actually on her mind and not in her spleen. So far, B.J. is still around.

Successful leaders know how to criticize their subordinates by packaging the criticism with a few compliments.

To be praised for a job well done helps cushion the blow when there is a postscript added suggesting that some aspects of the performance need improvement. It's hard to get angry when somebody has just told you that you are one of the firm's best lawyers.

Roger Craig, the manager of the San Francisco Giants, has a superb technique for handling the sensitive egos of his ballplayers. Even while he is pulling a pitcher out of a game, Craig is telling the guy he knows that next time he'll be a winner. It's humiliating to be taken off the mound in front of thousands of people. But there are tactful and diplomatic ways to let the guy know that tomorrow is another day.

Man-to-Man

A man can find another man to tell him how badly he's screwed up. And we do look for that sort of postgame analysis from male colleagues and friends. It's helpful to know how a competitor—and we are always in competition with other men—would have handled the same circumstance. But only a woman can tell a man that he is still her man, not a stockbroker who shouldn't have sold short when the market was turning long, not a professional ballplayer who didn't make the out, not a mechanic who's received a pink slip.

This support is what binds a couple together when there is trouble. It gives the woman credibility and leverage for offering advice that might otherwise be too painful or personal for the man to handle.

Initially, what he needs is comfort, support, and a lot of "I love you's" and "No matter what happens I'm with you and behind you's." The response will vary depending on the individual. Some men will pull back and spend time alone. Others tell me that they prefer to go off with the "boys" for a while. In either case, it should not be seen as a rejection of your love and support.

Once the sinking feeling has been stabilized, the practical aspects of picking up the pieces can be addressed. He values your opinion and independent judgment of a situation, but it goes beyond cold logic. If he says he is a failure on the job, he is asking you to rush the cavalry in for the rescue. He really needs you to tell him that the one thing he isn't is a failure. Maybe, along the way, he will get the idea that you need emotional first aid sometimes too.

There is room for concrete suggestions: "Honey, I wonder if it isn't time for you to think about a new career. This one just isn't working out. But whatever you decide to do, you can count on me." Job burnout happens all the time, and men fear the unknown because it could mean a change in social and economic status. He may worry that you will leave him if there is a drastic change. It may mean cutting back on your life-style, but, if the relationship is important, give him the support he needs to do what has to be done.

CHAPTER FOUR

EGO IS EVERYTHING

Poker parties are great places for picking up bits and pieces of wisdom. Dale loves to play cards, and I depend on him to keep on losing and listening. It was about two in the morning when this one dropped: "Men only want two things out of life—to get laid and to get a job," the dealer said, and nobody at the table (they were all men) bothered to argue the point, although the guy to the dealer's right chimed in with, "And to keep on getting laid and to keep on getting paid."

Dale walked out of there fifty dollars in the hole, but it was worth it. I could have spent a month dissecting Freudian theories to demonstrate why sex and the job are central to the strength of men's egos. Instead, I had a workable beer-and-pizza version of Freud thanks to Dale's weakness for bluffing when it's time to fold, and folding when it's time to bluff.

Cut from the smoke-filled room to scene two: the office of a pharmaceuticals executive. Joan is at her desk, speaking into the phone. She is talking to me.

"I like him a lot. We spend most of our free time together."

I listened to the preliminaries and asked, "So what's the problem?"

"The problem," she said, "is that when we're in bed he is a good lover, a considerate lover, and a sensitive lover, but . . ."

I saw where she was headed and cut her off. "Joan, is the next word you're about to give me *boring*?"

She didn't hesitate. Joan is used to my bluntness, and you probably are too by this point. "You bet. He is boring . . . borrrring in the sack," was her answer. "And what can I do about it?"

We ended up talking for an hour and a half, but I will boil down my advice to a few paragraphs. I started by telling Joan to remember that the way to a man's heart is through his ego. All human beings have egos; we are all ego-oriented. The truth of the matter is that most guys invest their ego in two specific areas: one, the job; two, the bed.

With this in mind, very specifically what needs to be done if you want a sensitive, considerate, thoughtful lover is to let him know that you believe he is one red-hot lover. Think back to the first time the two of you made love. I doubt that there would have been an encore if he had left you cold. Now do the easiest thing in the world. Just tell him how great it was (read on, and you will see that there is an immediate payoff).

The results are that his ego gets fired up again, he's excited, and he begins to feel like he is one hell of a man and one hell of a lucky guy to have you on his side. He imagines a direct link between you and his success as a lover. Children hear praise constantly and it nourishes their self-esteem. Positive reinforcement isn't as readily available to adults—and certainly not when it comes to sex. It has a tremendous impact.

This positive reinforcement generates its own reward. She who ignites the sexual bonfire gets to enjoy the heat.

I don't want to get too graphic (that's a job for your imagination), but if he has a great-looking body, compliment him. If his shoulders are a turn-on, let him know it. Say the words. If you get your lover excited, he will excite you.

Bravo! You've just set off every smoke detector in the house.

His Need to Know

Let's get Joan off the line and make a quick switch from the bedroom to the boardroom before I start sounding like a sex therapist. A man's ego—the same ego that can make the difference between a boring lover and a blazing lover—also draws strength from the job.

Men are taught that their role in life is to be the breadwinner. While women are certainly members in good standing of the work-a-day chain gang, men feel that their earning power is the central factor of their existence. I'm talking about conditioning, the incalculable number of subliminal messages that have been passed down to men since birth—and also over the last twenty-five million years.

Like the prescription I suggested for curing Joan's bedtime boredom, women who deliberately plug into a man's job-ego power grid, supplying extra juice—encouragement, suggestions, praise, interest—can energize those men and their relationships with them.

Boost his ego. Boost it just the way you did in bed when you told him that his lovemaking was like a Beethoven symphony. Let him know that you believe he is as much a genius in the nine-to-five world, the world of high pressure and deadlines, as he is in the private world of love and passion that the two of you share.

This doesn't mean that you have to patronize him, or that your career isn't important. Of course it is. But he needs to know that his contribution is recognized and valued.

Ego is not a dirty word. But it is a misunderstood word. The term is a label for the control mechanism that keeps our personalities balanced between the most primitive requirements of the psyche (sex being one of them) and the demands of the social and physical world around us. It gives us a sense of who we are. To put it more exactly, my ego tells me who "I" am, where "I" am, why "I" am.

If we were built like an automobile engine, the ego would be similar to the carburetor, which links the gas pedal and the pistons, harmonizing internal and external forces. Unfortunately, we can't lift the hood every five thousand miles and tinker with our psychological "carburetor" to keep it running smoothly.

The potholes of life take a toll on the ego. Strong and self-confident men can be left wondering if there's any point to getting out of bed in the morning and going to the office. Most of the things we do every day subject our egos to a hard pounding. There's the daily commuter grind that exposes us to strangers who seem ready and willing to kill us before we've had a second cup of coffee; the customer who refuses to answer phone calls; the client who screams that the bill is too high; copy machines designed to destroy documents; telephones designed to disconnect very important people; food designed to cause indigestion. No wonder that at about the age of forty many people encounter the infamous mid-life crisis. The ego, the sense of who "I" am, gets badly bent out of shape.

As children, if we were lucky enough to have wise and

loving parents, our young egos were constantly being rein-
forced and strengthened. There was praise and cuddling
for mastering the simplest acts. Suddenly, that all came to
an end. We grew up. Now it can be difficult to get so much
as a thank-you for beating the world with one hand and
slaying dragons with the other three times a day, five days
a week.

I put such heavy emphasis on boosting your man's ego
because if you don't do it, who will? He needs to know
that there is a "there, there." And because of your special
relationship with him, you know the "I" of the man better
than any boss or drinking pal.

If this book were about women and written for men, I
would also advise men to give the women in their lives
ego-booster shots. We need a buddy system: You massage
my ego, and I'll massage yours.

There are obvious practical benefits for women. When
he is feeling down, there is a danger he will pull you down
too, so crank him back up. Simple words—such as "You're
the best in the business"—can be a real tonic to a guy who
is feeling rotten about his job. And you'll find that with
his renewed and vigorous self-confidence, he'll be there
for you when things aren't going your way.

Investing in His Self-esteem

You may be saying at this point, as Joan did when I suggested she tell her lover what a turn-on he was, that it
seems kind of phony; isn't it just a lot of ego-stroking and
flattery? And that's a reasonable question. But in response,
let me offer the example of an attractive woman who would
like to be a little more attractive. She puts on some eye
liner, blush on her cheeks; maybe for good measure base

is applied and the eyebrows are touched up. And while her brown hair is nice, maybe some blond highlights might not be so bad. Once her hair has been dyed, it's time to work on the body: a little padding on the shoulders might be helpful.

Now, is she being phony? Joan didn't think so. She told me that the makeup, hair frosting, and padding were merely enhancing the woman's looks, enhancing what was already there. And I contend that enhancing a man's ego, enhancing what is already there inside him, is exactly the same thing.

The net result is this: You give a man confidence to be a man by letting him know that, in your book, in these two crucial areas—in the bedroom and at work—he is a gold medalist every time.

I'm not talking about feeding a man's ego to the point that he has to start paying excess baggage charges when he gets on an airplane: "Sorry, sir. You'll have to check your ego. It won't fit in the overhead rack."

The funny thing about human beings is that when we feel good about ourselves, when our self-esteem is riding high, everybody around us benefits—particularly those we love and those we are close to. I promise you, it will be the cheapest, most productive investment you will ever make in your life. No stock, no bond, no CD, will ever pay the kind of interest on the small investment that you will make in this area.

If he feels good about himself when it comes to sex and the job, those two acutely vulnerable zones, it will come back to you in spades. And the bonus is that he may also get the idea that you have ego needs as well. Feeling good about his ego, he will feel free to, in turn, boost your ego.

I will not attempt to identify the source of a woman's inner strength and self-confidence. My job, in this book, is to explain what makes men tick, and that is difficult enough, thank you. It is the reason I have focused on sex and the job as such major ego factors. I want women to understand how vitally important these areas are to men and to understand that men are different. There—I've said it again—different.

Giving Him a Booster Shot

Nancy Glass is a husband bragger—and most men love husband braggers. You've probably seen Nancy on TV; she's had a string of successful shows that have been chock-full of information and entertainment value. Whenever I talk to Nancy about her husband, a wonderful expression comes over her face and she can't say enough complimentary things about him. It's great. What a lucky guy!

Men are suckers for cheerleaders. Merrilee and Bob joke about Merrilee actually having been a cheerleader in college, but she still knows how to root for the home team. A few years ago, she was interviewed by her hometown newspaper in northern Maryland. The journalist wanted a local-girl-makes-good story and, as the director of news for three of ABC Radio's six networks, Merrilee filled the bill. As the interview progressed and she started to talk about how important her husband was to her professional life and what she loved about him, Bob, who was sitting in on the interview, felt wonderful. Talk about ego boosts. And if he feels wonderful about himself, it only makes sense that Bob is going to feel the same about her.

Couples tend to have trouble when self-esteem is at a low ebb. Men start to look for it from other women, other activities—a career change, maybe—just as you might under similar circumstances. But if we, as men, can get a self-esteem–booster shot at home from the women we love, believe me, it will help strengthen the relationship.

Being a Best Friend

My specialty is writing and talking about men. The subject doesn't mix particularly well with politics (what does?), but I can't resist tipping my hat to Jimmy Carter. Jimmy who?

That's right, Jimmy Carter. He was the first president to say that his wife was his best friend. These days, it doesn't seem like a revolutionary statement, but 1600 Pennsylvania Avenue had been the ultimate good old boy's clubhouse since John Adams, the mansion's first occupant, took up residence. Abigail Adams, and other first ladies, have had significant roles, but their influence was always treated like a curiosity, an indiscretion, or a presidential character flaw to be winked at by political allies and whispered about by adversaries.

Jimmy Carter took the unusual step of actually putting his wife on the public Oval Office schedule for a weekly *working* luncheon. Until the press got used to the idea, spokesman Jody Powell was pestered with questions about the kind of advice the First Lady dared to offer her husband at those sessions. And Rosalynn Carter was indeed a valued adviser to the president. She served as a roving ambassador on several important foreign missions.

I'm convinced that a lot of Jimmy Carter's quiet inner strength was a direct result of his partnership with Rosalynn. He knew that she would always be there. He could count on her. In an emergency, Jimmy had a best friend in his corner. And there were emergencies, severe trials and tribulations; through it all, the friendship endured.

I always felt that Jimmy was Rosalynn's hero, as corny as it may sound. But what's so corny about heroes? I hope that I am my wife's hero. She's mine; I'm proud of what she's accomplished and how far she has gone professionally. But the mutual admiration society does not mean that one of us has to be put down so that the other can be up on a pedestal. Never make that mistake; there's room enough for two up there. But help him strengthen his ego, and he will repay that investment no matter what happens to the Dow Jones Industrial Average.

CHAPTER FIVE

BIG SPORTS

Question: Why do men get angry when you beat them at Ping-Pong?

Answer: In some states beating your husband at Ping-Pong is grounds for divorce. No, that's not true. Ping-Pong is just one of the hundreds of competitive activities that men think they should be good at. Parents, teachers, our friends, the books we read, television shows, and women—that's right, women—have all helped persuade us that as men we're good at throwing a ball and swinging a bat. Or swinging a hammer. Mr. Fix-it, the home handyman, is as enduring a myth as Little Red Ridinghood. But I know men who get the cold sweats just thinking about changing the washer on a dripping faucet.

When he can't smash the ball over the net, pound the nail, stop the leak, he feels that he has failed as a "man." Is this a silly attitude? Yes, it is. But that's the reason that the last time you beat him at Ping-Pong he threw the paddles out the window.

Women aren't totally immune to this sort of thing. I know an older couple who have been happily married for years. They're both excellent gardeners, but he rarely visits the flower beds or the vegetable patch anymore because he learned early on that it was her turf. When he pruned or weeded there was always something wrong, as far as she was concerned. He was playing her game and winning; and she didn't like it.

Theoretically, freedom of the garden and freedom of the Ping-Pong table are inalienable American rights, but in practice it's not so easy. Maybe Harry Truman had it right: "If you can't stand the heat, get out of the kitchen [or the garden]." That's what my friend does. He has opted not to compete with his wife. She grows the flowers and the vegetables, and he admires them.

But I don't know whether I like that idea. If you want to play Ping-Pong or whatever, play it. If he loses, give him ego reinforcement in other areas. Don't gloat or lord it over him when you win. On the other hand, don't deliberately throw the game. Losing fair and square is bad enough. Winning because your opponent took pity really hurts.

Some people would say that the relationship is all that counts and that taking a dive to soothe his ego is smart. It may be smart, but it's definitely phony. In the last chapter I advised you to put "makeup" on your relationship in order to enhance what's already there. I didn't say to put a false face on it.

Question: Why do men make such a big deal about sports?

Answer: First of all, spectator sports are male soap opera. A lot of women get hooked on soaps—the plots, the characters, the intrigue. It's the same thing with sports. There's a beginning, a middle, and, with any luck, a good climax. And that's the long and short of it. It's escapism, it's entertainment, it's a way of getting away from the BS in your life.

Sports is also a form of male bonding. Competition, and here I'm talking about participating in sports, does not alienate men from each other; it brings them closer together. I've known vicious competitors in the business world who respected each other and in time became the best of friends. I've seen it in boxing. Here are two guys swapping blows for fifteen rounds, and at the end they hug each other and mean it. The competition has created a bond.

Competition is king for men. They depend on it for shaping their identity, for stimulation and challenge. When I knock Craig down and step on his face, there's nothing personal in it. Craig knows that and he'll return the favor as soon as he gets up out of the mud.

TV sports appeals to men by way of this ongoing interest in competition while encouraging passivity and inactivity. Hours are wasted in front of a television set each weekend. But it's not exclusively a male problem. Men and women are hooked on TV. The daytime television network audience is predominately female. The majority of viewers in evening prime time are also women. In his book *Super Marital Sex: Loving for Life*, Dr. Paul Pearsall contends that television has been one of the greatest hindrances to healthy marriages. Couples will come home after a day at work: "Hi, how are you?" "Fine, and you?" "Great." Then it's off to the TV for the rest of the night.

Phil Donahue has a good line about men who are TV sportsaholics. The only way his wife could tell that old Mel was dead "was that when ESPN went off the air for the night he didn't budge from his easy chair."

The men I know who actively participate in sports tend to watch fewer hours of sports TV, and run less risk of ending up like old Mel. They just don't have enough time to shoot baskets, jog in marathons, or golf and also flake out in front of the tube. Therefore, a man's competitive instinct may be the key to breaking the TV habit. If he is out on the tennis court or the ball field—and you are there with him—sports can stimulate an "action cycle" that works as an antidote to the numbing effect of constant television watching.

The occasional binge of sports TV isn't all bad. Museums and concert halls are pleasantly uncrowded on Superbowl Sunday. If he is glued to his chair watching every pass, punt, and kick, join him for a little video togetherness; you may discover that you enjoy the spectacle. Otherwise, there's plenty of time for sewing, shopping, and get-togethers with friends.

Question: Why do men go hunting?

Answer: I'm not comfortable with hunting. I'm a city kid and I've never understood the thrill of shooting an animal. But I don't want to be too hypocritical and call the sport barbaric because I do eat meat and wear leather.

For many young men and boys, hunting is a rite of passage. When a father takes his son out hunting for the first time, there is a ritual going on that is rooted deeply in our past. It goes back thousands of years. Not much is said while you're hunting; the words are irrelevant between father and son while they are in the woods and fields. There's a telescoping of the generations. Dad is reliving his youth and that long-ago first day in the woods with his father, and the son is receiving a gift of time and experience that takes him a step closer to adulthood.

Real hunters—not the trendy outdoors type or the gun nuts—are seeking a closeness with nature. They become one with their prey. You can't get it any other way. Picture taking is fun, but it's not the same. Carnivores are hunters by instinct and necessity. Men who hunt are out to capture that primitive state of existence as both man and animal.

I'm still not at ease with the idea of killing for sport, but after a trip to Vermont where I did a story on hunting for the *Today* show, I began to understand what is taking place when we hear the guns of autumn in the distance.

Male bonding is a term that's tossed around and overused to the point that it's subject to ridicule. I once saw a cartoon depicting two men beating each other's brains out, and a woman bystander says, "Oh, they're engaged in male bonding." But laughs aside, there is something to male bonding. Men spending time with other men, cooperating, competing, developing friendships, is at the core of hunting.

Even if the rifle or shotgun is never fired, the hunting trip can be a success. The old maxim "It's not whether you win or lose, but the way you play the game" has a special meaning for those who rise before dawn to go deep into the woods. The hours of solitude are as important as the fraction of a second that it takes to pull the trigger. The hunter, alone with himself, taps into an individuality that sets him apart from the family or tribe. When he returns from the hunt, the hunter is a different man.

Man, modern man, is a communal creature. But when

he hunts, a man goes it alone. He succeeds or fails solely on his own luck and skill.

The animals stalked by our forefathers taught them how to think in a logical cause-and-effect manner. And although today's hunter may be a computer engineer, he is exercising mental powers that are the very foundation of his highest intellectual attainments. He is returning to the source of his own humanity when he whistles for his dog and heads into the wind on a gray November day.

Those who have looked down the barrel of a rifle or along the shaft of an arrow, aligning their sights on a living creature, say there is a rush of adrenaline that sets off a physical reaction the likes of which they have never experienced from any other activity, not from sex, driving at high speeds, or parachuting out of airplanes.

You may object to blood sports, but what I saw that day in Vermont seemed to be more sustaining ritual than frivolity.

Question: Why do men prefer to be behind the wheel of a car rather than between the sheets?

Answer: I've got to be real careful with this one. It's a classic have-you-stopped-beating-your-wife's-Corvette question. In our American folklore, the ideal man is the cowboy. He is independent and roams the wide world by himself. Well, a car gives a man that same sense of independence. He is his own man and not controlled by someone else. It gives him a chance to be in charge. Of course, when the monthly payments fall due, the bank is in charge.

Driving skillfully is fun, and there is always an element

of danger that provides a guy with a nice hit of adrenaline after a day cooped up in the office. And cars are relatively basic devices; you point them in the right direction and step on the gas. It is a simple pleasure in a complicated world.

CHAPTER SIX

YOU'RE FIRED

Outplacement. Now, there's a real Frankenstein of a word. Like death (passed away; gone to his reward) and taxes (revenue enhancement; user fees), I guess we needed a high-tech euphemism to soften the blow when the ax falls.

"Sorry, you're . . . outplaced as of Friday."

An industry is developing—outplacement counseling —to help men say the words—"I got fired today"—and live with the consequences. But it will never be easy. When he is fired, a man loses hold of his culturally implanted *raison d'être.* Forget about the obvious stuff: loss of income, embarrassment, uncertainty about the future. The core of his self-image is gone. The reason (his reason) for being here on earth has been taken away from him.

He may be a lover, a husband, a father, a brother, a valued member of the community; but without the job he has been cut adrift. Over the last ten years we've seen it happen in Youngstown and Detroit, the farm belt and the oil patch.

Doing versus Being

Why can't men keep their jobs in perspective?

Lane, an oil-drilling platform worker from Louisiana, probably had the best answer to that question. He said, "I can remember the first 'adult' conversation I had when I was a little one. It was the man from down the road was at our house—and he asked me what I was going to do when I grew up. I don't know what I told him, probably be Davy Crockett or a cowboy. But that's what it's all about. What are you going to *do* when you grow up?"

How's that again? Who are you going to be? No . . . what are you going to do?

Women are asked the same question, and the outplacement counselors expect a growing number to join the programs as women move into middle management, a zone that traditionally yields some of the highest corporate casualty rates. But I want to keep the focus on men in order to drive home the point that job loss to a man is a major crisis, probably *the* major crisis in his life.

Pink Slips and Pink Slippers

Once in a while the rumor goes around—and it's surely just a rumor—that there are some women who are attracted to men because of the money they make or their impressive job titles. Most other men have heard the same rumor, and when we lose a job, we also fear that we've lost our attractiveness to the women in our lives. In other words, without the job we're nothing.

In his book *Brown's Guide to Growing Gray*, David Brown has a variation on the familiar elderly Hollywood mogul with a taste for younger women. He credits the comedian Myron Cohen for the punchline. "Darling, if I lost all my money would you still love me?" "Of course I would," the Lolita replied, "and I would miss you."

Expressing Your Anger

When Alex was fired, his wife, Trish, made it a point not to talk about what was going on in her office. In that way, there was no painful reminder that he was stuck at home, without an office, a desk, a place to go when he woke up in the morning. It was a tactful thing to do, and if Alex asked a direct question about her business activities, he would get a direct answer. She just didn't hit him over the head with his situation.

Naturally, Trish was concerned and anxious about money. They had lost more than half their income. There were mortgages and bills to be paid. But she never made him squirm. If she was angry about it—and I'm sure she was—she bit her tongue. Maybe she went to a friend to sound off, but Alex didn't hear about it.

There are several outlets for venting your frustration. A normally easygoing producer at NBC tells me that she waits for her husband to leave the apartment and then takes off her shoes, grabs one of his suits from the closet, and stomps on it. Well . . . whatever works.

Don't express your anger to him. Now is not the time. His ego is damaged enough as it is. Help rebuild that ego.

Encouraging the Discouraged

A man's goal-oriented biases can be put to work constructively. Urge him to start the day, or prepare for it the night before, by listing everything he should be doing to get his career back on track. It can be something as basic as: (1) Go to the newsstand for the paper; (2) Read the help-wanted ads; (3) Retype resume . . . etc. One step at a time. There may be twenty-five items on the list, and at the end of the day, if he has checked off the majority, he will feel a sense of accomplishment. It is a slow rebuilding process. He needs to know that he is gaining back control.

Avoiding Controversy

Marital problems can start mushrooming during a job crisis. Unemployed men start to feel trapped and jumpy. The best thing for you to do during this period is to avoid controversy. As hard as it may be—and it will be hard—duck the issue when sore subjects come up. There will be time later, when he's back on the job, to have your say.

Until the crisis is over, he needs support and guidance. Be a sounding board for his ideas. Keep the pressure from escalating so that he can concentrate on the job of finding a job.

CHAPTER SEVEN

JERKS "R" US

Why are men such jerks? I've been asked the question so many times that I hear it in my sleep.

Answer (while asleep):

1. To irritate women.
2. We can't help ourselves.
3. It's something we ate.
4. Women expect jerks, so they get jerks.
5. Survival of the fittest, and jerks are survivors.
6. Jerks have more fun.
7. To be a jerk is human, and that includes women.
8. Jerks get laid.
9. Name a great man, and I'll show you a jerk. Gandhi? He never changed his underwear.
10. Nobody's perfect.

So all I've proven, you say, is that I am a jerk (while asleep). And I plead guilty to the charge. The truth of the matter is that part of being a guy is being a jerk. I don't think it's such a bad thing.

Do you? But before you answer that question, I've got to pose another: What is a jerk?

Since this is a book about men, the answer should come from men. The dozen guys I asked recognized that women regard them as jerks, but they couldn't agree on the definition. The answers ranged from being a slob and stubborn to forgetting birthdays and showing up late for a date. One gave me a variation on Dorothy Parker's idea of a gentleman: A jerk is a guy who forgets to put half of his weight on his elbows while making love.

With a spread as wide as that, I think I will forget the definition and go with: I know one when I see one.

When I talk to women about this, it becomes clear that the element of jerkiness, when it's not carried to extremes, of course, is part of what is appealing; it's part of our charm. There was a case in point from television: Why would prim-and-proper Maddie Hayes have had the hots for not-so-prim-or-proper and quintessential jerk David Addison on the ABC show *Moonlighting*? Was it because David had so much money? No, she was the boss and he worked for her. Was it because he was so good-looking? No, David was okay but not classically, Hollywood handsome. It's because he was a jerk. David was a 100 percent jerk. His role model was Curly of the Three Stooges. Maddie had been getting a hard time from him for years. He acted like a jerk, was a wiseass (but he was also into commitment, by the way), and big trouble. It drove Maddie crazy and she loved him madly.

Even so, the scriptwriters didn't even come close to capturing the electricity of the classic beauty-and-the-beast combination that occurred when Lauren Bacall was paired off with Humphrey Bogart. Bacall's "If you want me, just whistle" sent millions of male and female movie fans right up the theater walls with the hots. Bogart became an archetypal jerk on the loose, roaming the Petrified Forest, running rapids in *The African Queen*, managing a gin mill in Casablanca.

Sandra Bernhard, the comedienne, said in an interview, "I dig Letterman [David] because he is so hard to get to." Translate the comment and what do we get? He acts like a jerk. It may frustrate her and drive her crazy, but it also seems to interest her.

Dare I say that there is a little-boy quality to the jerk without giving ammunition to those whose favorite put-down is: "See! Men won't grow up. They can't grow up!"

We get into trouble by thinking that there is such a thing as being "grown up." When does it happen? The first lie? The first love? A doctor's prognosis that the cancer is terminal? Without a clearly marked threshold between being a child and being grown up, we are left to concoct an ideal grown-up man and an ideal grown-up woman. We keep running after these role models, but they have the maddening habit of receding like mirages.

It is frustrating, and out of that frustration the jerk is born.

Looking Beneath the Dignified Surface

When I was on *Donahue* a few years ago, Phil gave the audience his favorite routine about men. He calls it the young male at a baseball game. He's with a bunch of his buddies, they're drinking beer—not the standard can of beer but a thirty-two-ounce bucket—and you get a "UUUUUGH HEEEEEEY OOOuuugh" kind of noise from the bleachers. Phil provided all the sound effects and the gestures. The message was that these males are subhuman.

While we were on the air, I suggested to Phil that drinking beer at the ball park is not a big deal. I'd hate to think that young Phil Donahue never had the fun of being a jerk every now and then. Just as I hate to think that the grown-up Donahue is so successful he can't take a chance on being joyously jerky.

A few days after the show, invitations went out to the joyous and the jerky to take part in a rib-eating contest at baseball celebrity Rusty Staub's Manhattan restaurant. There I was, on the posh Upper East Side, surrounded by the city's professional athletic elite and feeling as out of place as George Bush would at a rap-music fest. But as soon as one of Rusty's gorgeous ladies tied the bib around my neck, I was a little boy again, and did I ever make a fool out of myself (I came in third, and would have placed higher had I not lost valuable seconds chewing on the tip of my right thumb). It was great—Jerks "R" Us—fun.

Grabbing a Hunk

In *The Washington Post* I saw a small news item about a guy who was taking a year off from his life to become a "Hunk." He moved from Atlanta to the Bahamas and wanted to revamp his body and his image totally in one year. He was fat, bald, forty-five, and not very attractive in the Hollywood sense. My eyes lit up. Jackpot! Remar "Bubba" Sutton was the jerk I had been looking for.

I drove back to New York that same day, and the first thing the next morning I went to my boss's office to sell him on the idea. I'm charging toward the door and I freeze in my tracks. Wait a minute, I thought to myself. Suppose he takes this the wrong way? My boss was overweight, wore glasses, and nobody was going to confuse Steve Friedman with Robert Redford. I wondered if I was leaving myself open to the charge that I was mocking men who are chunky and not beach-boy handsome. But it was too late to stop, and Steve immediately saw Bubba's potential.

As a result, I got the chance to accompany Bubba part of the way on what he called his "march to macho." It was a lot of fun. I did three *Today* show stories—sort of a beginning, middle, and end approach. And the viewers could watch Bubba transform himself into a hunk and participate in his fantasy.

He lost weight, built up his muscles with a rigorous training program, consulted with plastic surgeons and hair-transplant specialists, and jazzed up his wardrobe. In the Bahamas and California, Bubba perfected his "swoon walk." He'd stroll down the beach trying to drive the women crazy. And, believe it or not, he got a lot of noise from them—some appreciative, some not so appreciative. You can't please everybody, after all.

In short, it was not the kind of behavior you'd expect from a solid, respectable middle-aged man. Only a jerk could have set out to become a "Hunk."

And do you know what? People loved it. We got an unbelievable reaction from the audience. Jane Pauley, the show's co-anchor, came back from trendy Manhattan cocktail parties saying that she had been bombarded with questions about the "Hunk." "How's Bubba?" "Is he for real?" "When's he going to be on next?"

We like jerks; we like being jerks.

And as a postscript, Bubba may be a jerk, but he's no fool. His "march from chunk to hunk" led to a book, a syndicated newspaper column, and a movie deal.

Single Women and Married Men

I hosted a television show not long ago, and I asked women in the audience to share some of their "jerk" experiences. There are topics that fall flat, but this one sure didn't. I could have done a miniseries and called it *Jerks du jour*.

The very first woman to stand up said she had been dating a guy for three months before she realized that he was married. At that point, instead of telling him to take a hike, she bought his line that he was planning to get a divorce. Of course, it never happened.

He was a jerk. I agree. But what about her? Men can be good at lying, but not that good. There is no such thing as a perfect liar. Three months of an intimate relationship went by, and she still had not figured out what was happening? I suspect that she didn't want to know.

When we deny reality, we are protecting ourselves from its pain. Nobody wants to be hurt, and denial is a perfectly understandable reaction. Understandable, but dangerous. Little things have a way of disappearing when they are ignored; it's the big stuff that hangs on and gets worse.

Dating a man and neglecting to find out whether he is married or single rates as "big stuff." The marriage is not going to go away just because it's ignored. Naïveté may be responsible for some shortsightedness. We've all been naïve at one point or another. Even so, when I meet women who spend their professional lives negotiating rock-solid contracts or clinching million-dollar computer deals, the "I guess I was naïve" routine starts to sound slightly hollow.

There is a terrific scene in the film *A Guide for the Married*

Man. The character played by Joey Bishop is in bed with another woman, and his wife barges into the room. As I remember the dialogue, it went something like this:

She says, "What are you doing with that woman?!!"

Bishop looks over and asks, "What woman?"

"That woman . . . the one in bed."

"I don't know what you're talking about."

Bishop and the bimbo get out of bed and dress while the wife yells, "That woman, the one that's getting dressed."

Bishop's girlfriend walks out the door, finally. It's a very long and funny scene, played for maximum laughs. In the end, Bishop asks his wife whom she is going to believe, him or her own eyes. The wife looks into the camera in utter astonishment and confusion.

Believe your eyes.

A man and a woman exchange business cards. He says, "Only call me at the office." And she asks why. "Oh, my place is being renovated and I'm living with my elderly parents."

Do you hear the warning bells? Believe your ears. And women have told me these kinds of stories without the slightest indication of even beginning to grasp what's going on. They look shocked when I burst the bubble and say, "He's married!" "Married?" "Yes, married!"

However, I don't want to encourage overreaction. Assuming that a man is lying whenever he opens his mouth is not going to solve anything. Blind jealousy toward a husband or a lover will damage a relationship just as much as blind faith. Let common sense and hard evidence dictate your actions. Don't imagine things, but don't let the obvious slip right by.

"Who are you going to believe, me or your eyes?"

Believe your eyes.

Enjoying a Jerk

Men have split personalities. On one side of the coin there is "Hawkeye" Pierce of *M*A*S*H*, the hardworking, sensitive doctor; on the other side is "Hawkeye" Pierce, the gin-swilling playboy out to score with the nurses. Clint Eastwood is the latest of a long line of "reel men." As "Dirty Harry," a take-charge guy, masculine and quiet, he doesn't tell you what he feels; he shows you. There's no doubt how Clint Eastwood feels when he is up there on the screen (naturally, I'm talking about the stock Clint Eastwood character; it's a mistake to confuse the actor with the characters he plays).

A good insight on jerks comes from Bobbie Moran, a staff writer for the *San Diego Union*: "My mom says that when men get to be about eight years old, they enter a goony stage that they don't outgrow until they are about sixty-five. She says this with great affection, of course, since the very fact that men will be boys is part of their charm." And Ms. Moran adds a kicker to her newspaper column: "But in husband hunting, charm can often get in the way of reality."

I'll second the motion, although there needs to be an amendment attached. Growing up isn't easy for men or women. As I noted earlier in the chapter, since there is no set point when childhood ends and grown-uphood begins, we are left groping for the grown-up ideal. Is a grown-up a joyless drudge, someone who never makes mistakes, a martyr? The process is always incomplete, and there is a child within all of us. The urge to go back and recapture the feelings of love and security we felt as children never completely fades away. As a spouse or lover, living within the intimate zones of another person's life, you should expect to see some lightning flashes of immaturity on occasion.

The charmer, the jerk, the goon, may get in the way of reality. But he is also showing you a side of the "real" man, rather than a piece of sculpture that's too good to be true.

CHAPTER EIGHT

DATING

Dating is often a dress rehearsal for marriage, or an undress rehearsal. And to keep the theatrical theme going, remember Flip Wilson's all purpose one-liner—"What you see is what you get."

It always knocks me out when women say to me, "I wish my husband could express his feelings." I count slowly to ten before I respond: "Did he express his feelings when you were dating?" There's usually a moment or two of verbal tap dancing: ". . . a little"; ". . . sometimes"; ". . . well, not a lot." Eventually, we get around to the real answer, which is—"No."

Now, there's a follow-up question: "What made you think that he was going to change once you got married?"

Some women fall into the trap of what my friend Dr. Georgia Witkin calls falling in love with a man's potential. To a person lost in the desert, the palm trees and babbling brook in the distance are a potential oasis and a probable mirage. Think of his potential as a mirage. It could be the real thing, but don't throw away your water bottle.

We all rebel against our parents to one degree or another. But, while it's a cliché, there is a lot of truth to the old saw "The apple doesn't fall far from the tree." If you've met his father, and the old man is an "old man" (in the sense of attitudes toward women), don't be surprised if the son reflects many of those same values. And if he is actively rebelling against "Daddy Dearest," the enlightened veneer that so charmed you could eventually wear off. The reverse is also true. Donna persuaded herself that Jim's business "style"—curt, aggressive, and short on good manners—did not represent the man that she was beginning to admire. And Jim could be charming in a social situation with Donna. Six or seven months into the relationship, she began to realize that her lover was indeed curt, aggressive, and short on good manners. The charming Jim wasn't the real Jim. She should have been on guard after seeing him in action on the job.

The urge to hope for the best is powerfully seductive, but there's an eleventh commandment (or is it the twelfth?) that can keep you out of trouble: Thou shalt not kid thyself. He is what he is. Changing another person's well-established behavior patterns is extremely difficult, and it is not a pleasant process for the changer or the changee.

Competition Is Harmful to a Relationship

Dating is not an Olympic sport. Being a friend and lover is difficult enough, but combining love, friendship, and competition fundamentally alters a relationship, straining it to the breaking point.

I know a woman who is a psychologist—so she's supposed to know better—and she told me that she once challenged a guy she was dating to a driving contest. She wanted to prove to him that women are better drivers than men. I asked her if he was making it an issue. She said, "Oh, no. I just thought it would be kind of fun."

She called it fun! I call it a mistake. He's got enough competition at the office. When he is with his woman, the last thing he wants is a contest.

The same woman has a habit of dropping bombshell comments. They are in the car, a Simon and Garfunkel tune is playing on the radio, and this prompts her to announce that Art Garfunkel once made a pass at her. A news story about Edward Kennedy triggers her revelation that Ted was also hot to trot. Was she telling the truth? Who cares. It's a form of competition that only hurts a relationship. You don't like it when he does it to you— so, understandably, he doesn't like it when you do it to him.

Of course, there are competition "junkies," people who can't help themselves. They crave the stimulation and the exhilarating highs generated by competing with others. Once again, if he is addicted to competition, you cannot cure or reform him. If you're the one who is hooked, it's important to understand that competitors always fall into two categories: winners and losers. In a close relationship shared by just two people, a competitive tug-of-war doesn't leave much room for compromise and conciliation. The result is a cold and unyielding formula—he wins, you lose; you win, he loses.

Men are just beginning to learn how to cope with competition from women in the workplace, and some of us are very slow learners. We've been going up against other males since childhood. It's second nature when *mano a mano* time comes—we know exactly what to expect—but when a woman is involved it's a whole new ball game. This may help explain why men sometimes deal with their female colleagues in such a clumsy way; and—yes—sometimes in a sexist, patronizing way. I'm not likely to use "sweety" and "honey" and other such cutesyness on someone I expect to knock me down, step on my face, and steal the million-dollar Allied Bellrope account.

Women are making men eat those words. And what I say to that is, "Right on!" But it would be a mistake to underestimate how well developed and crudely powerful the competitive instinct can be when it's aroused in men.

Until this century, when a man "took on the world," he was only battling half of it—other men. Now he really does fight on both fronts. It's comforting, for men and women, to have at least one demilitarized zone in our lives.

When you're in the office, go ahead—kick ass. At home, why not grab ass?

To Call or Not to Call

Has this happened to you? The party has been great; you've spent about two hours talking to a good-looking, interesting guy. Things are winding down and he asks for your phone number. No problem there. You hand over your business card, or jot down the number on a scrap of paper. He says he'll call in a few days. Terrific!

And you never hear from him.

It happens all the time. I've got a surefire technique for seeing that it never happens to you again. When he asks for the telephone number, give it to him and then get his number.

There is no stock reason to explain why guys don't call. He may have had second thoughts—maybe you're not his type after all. The recurring amnesia about his twenty-year marriage and three kids suddenly lifted. He was just being polite, figuring that you expected him to ask for the number. Perhaps he sent the scrap of paper to the dry cleaner with his blue blazer. A business or family crisis could have intervened.

A quick call from you after a few days have gone by would resolve the uncertainty. If he is no longer interested, the message will come through loud and clear. No harm done. If he is interested, so much the better. You win or break even.

There's another possibility. He may fear that when he calls he will hear something like this: "David . . . David . . . the one from Harvard or Georgetown?" Or: "Tell me what you were wearing."

Men fear rejection. And many times we take the easy way out to avoid it. Successful men have told me—and I am talking about guys who swing enormous influence— that the fear of being rejected by women is the worst feeling of all, and that it never gets any easier to take the risk, from that first time in seventh grade, asking the girl in math class to go to the square dance, to inviting the lady in the red dress to spend the weekend in Paris.

As we discussed earlier, this fear stems from the basic importance of sex to a man's ego. He feels exposed and vulnerable when he initiates a sexual encounter. Warren Farrell, the author and educator whom I mentioned in Chapter Three, conducts seminars in which men get to play the traditional female parts and women take over male social roles. Warren asks the men to stand up and turn around so that their bodies can be inspected from every angle. In his carefully orchestrated seminars, the women have to risk rejection by asking the guys to go out to dinner. It makes for a very insightful situation, and when I went through it, I could feel the power women have over men. (I first heard the term *success object* at one of Warren's seminars, a perfect way to raise the issue of women who lust after a man's material resources the way some men reduce women to the status of sex objects.)

The Invisible Chaperone

In real life, by taking some of the initiative, women share a portion of the risk. Yes, rejection hurts, but the tradeoff is that you gain more control over the dating mechanism.

Active, energetic, dynamic women come down with arthritis of the finger when they have to dial a man's telephone number. The malady leaves them in a frustrating and passive position.

It doesn't have to happen. Men are not as put off as you might think by "aggressive women." But let's stop and take a second look at that phrase—*aggressive women*—before we go on.

What are we talking about, anyway? Amazons? Ballbusters? Loose women? Uppity women? A working mother? A single parent? A woman at the head of a boardroom table?

The problem is that nontraditional, nonconventional, out-of-the-norm behavior by women has usually been written off as "aggressive." The stigma has made it difficult for women to break out of stereotypical roles. We are told that the stereotypes are breaking down: Look at *Cagney and Lacey*, the TV cops.

Down on the ground, though, these radical notions have been slower to evolve. The dating-and-mating dance, because it is largely conducted in private and without a chorus of social arbiters commenting at every turn, proceeds as though the maiden's chaperone might pop around the corner and catch her in the sin of holding hands.

For many men, being asked for a date by a woman comes as a surprise. The first time it happens, she is probably categorized as an "aggressive woman." After the second and third times, the aggressive woman is well on her way to becoming the contemporary woman.

This process of change can take place only if women assume the initiative. If you don't ask, you have to wait to be asked. The choice is passivity or action. As always, there is the risk of rejection and failure that goes with any decision to take action.

There is nothing particularly aggressive about calling someone and saying, "I've got a couple of tickets to the show. Are you interested?" There are men who may misinterpret the gesture or feel that they are losing control. Yet, I'd bet that if there is a spark of interest and attraction between the two of you, he won't slam down the phone and blush himself to sleep. He may have other plans. If he does, try again. And in the meantime, as the definition of *aggressive women* is being rewritten, he may call you with the news that he's come up with a couple of tickets to another show.

By and large, having the fear of rejection eased is such a plus for a man that the early awkward, tentative stages of a relationship—and we've all suffered through them—won't be quite so agonizing and accident-prone.

Your SDI: The Strategic Dating Initiative

I've observed a lot of modern women who are wonderful at coming up with strategies, enthusiasm, and commitment on behalf of advancing their careers. Or they do the impossible and find spectacular places to live in cities like New York, Philadelphia, or Chicago. Their creativity bubbles over and they turn up just the right inspired and beautifully packaged birthday present for a friend.

These women are alive in every way. Yet, where is the same spark when it comes to taking the initiative and meeting new men? The inspired strategizing that went into the apartment, the gift, the job, doesn't happen where men are involved. The results aren't surprising.

It may be, as one woman told me, that it comes down to "finding guys through happenstance." In Washington, D.C., happenstance can be the Georgetown Safeway, which has been nicknamed the "Single's Safeway" in recognition of the store's role as a meeting place for young professionals.

Want to meet men? Go grocery shopping. It's not a new idea, but there are some fresh refinements. Timing is important; late evening is best, when busy professionals finally get away from the office. Stake out the gourmet-food section and look for guys with interesting items in their carts; they're the ones who have outgrown TV dinners.

There are other ways beyond haunting supermarkets to meet men. Enroll in adult-education classes, which offer another relaxed, low-pressure setting. You'll meet new men, and they'll be men with whom you share a common interest. Signing on to help a political campaign will put you in contact with interesting men. Volunteer fire departments and rescue squads can always use another pair of hands. Ski trips, scuba-diving excursions, and business workshops are crawling with men. And here's the ultimate—a season ticket to the local team's home games.

Tina bought a house in the Washington suburbs. The place needed work and the home-improvement contractor she called for an estimate turned out to be an improvement on the so-called professional men she had been dating.

Tina fell in love with her home handyman and today they're married. Maybe she stumbled onto a new technique for meeting men: Get out the Yellow Pages, start with Appliance Repair, and work through to Window Replacement. At least he'll be able to use a screwdriver.

Airline clubs are the singles bars of the latter part of the twentieth century. They are great places to meet men. The setting is nonthreatening and there's none of this "You must be a pretty fast little number or you wouldn't be hanging around here" stuff. Exchanging business cards in an airline club while you're waiting to make connections (airline connections) is perfectly natural.

The old neighborhood pub is another place to go to meet men. I'm not talking about a singles meat rack. The place on the corner with the neon beer sign in the window will do just fine. Guys tell me that they meet some wonderful women in bars. It's comfortable, everybody's relaxed, there's no pressure to score.

The novel *Looking for Mr. Goodbar* did a real job on the singles-bar scene, but Jill, who is a media consultant in Dallas, tells me that she still makes an occasional foray into the city's singles bars. She takes a girlfriend along, and they usually end up talking to a couple of interesting men. It doesn't have to be a lifelong relationship, or even a romance. A few laughs over a drink can't hurt. And as Jill says, "Practice makes perfect." The more men you meet, the better you get at spotting the winners and the losers.

Pam lives in Manhattan and her technique is well adapted to that city. If it's raining she just waits under an awning; before long she's met two or three new guys. I tease her about praying for rain and deliberately leaving her umbrella at home.

Some men and women swear by personal ads. But

really think hard about the best way to describe yourself. Find a striking attribute that will generate interest. Don't bother with "I'm attractive . . . a good conversationalist . . . looking for an intelligent man . . ." That's boring. Come up with the one thing that makes you special, or focus on the elements that turn you on, or off, about a man. Amy, a veteran cabbie who knows every shortcut between O'Hare and the Palmer House, told me that her most successful ads always start with "WSF cab driver with an addiction for Laura Ashley clothes, big mongrel dogs, and the cello seeks a man who is willing to say yes to life and maybe to love." It happens to be a quick and accurate sketch of Amy, who is a sucker for the "British country look," keeps an enormous beast with her in the front seat of the cab to discourage unruly passengers, and plays the cello in a chamber group whenever she's not stuck in traffic.

Ads should be specific. And don't kid yourself, either. If you advertise for a guy who loves books and long walks in the country, you had better not be allergic to fresh air and first editions.

The same thing applies to painting a false picture of yourself in the ad. He'll know that he's been suckered in about five seconds flat after he sees you.

A final word about personal ads and personal safety. Hundreds of people, perhaps thousands, will read your ad. There is no way a publication can screen out the kooks, the cranks, and the crazies. For the first encounter, arrange to meet the person who responds to the ad someplace other than your apartment or house. Without taking this basic precaution, you could end up being harassed or in physical danger. Have him over for dinner on the second or third date. By then you'll know whether he is housebroken.

Gaffes Galore

First dates are tricky, and I don't think anybody ever really masters the technique. I have a friend who runs a hair-cutting salon, and I asked her to find out from the customers—male and female—what *not* to do on a first date.

Don't talk about old boyfriends or ex-husbands.

Don't give him the third degree about his former girl-friends (but if he raises the subject, listen closely).

Don't make a big thing about being on a diet, especially if he has taken you to a fancy restaurant.

Don't hire a financial rating service to do a background check (it's been done).

Don't look too surprised if he asks you to split the check (you're allowed to put it on your gold card, but don't smirk).

Don't forget your date's name.

If you do forget your date's name, don't admit it.

Don't lose a contact lens.

If you do lose a contact lens, don't get down on your knees in The Russian Tea Room to look for it. Write it off.

Don't ask the waiter for a doggy bag.

Don't ask him to ask the waiter for a doggy bag.

Don't laugh if he asks the waiter for a doggy bag without your asking him to ask.

Don't ask if he actually owns a dog.

While we are on the subject of first dates, I want to pass along a supposedly foolproof method for determining how good a guy will be in bed by watching the way he eats. Don't blame me if it doesn't work, though. I am merely the middleman on this one. Chris Scott claims it's very accurate, and I'm too much of a gentleman to ask her for specifics. She says to watch the way a man attacks his plate. If he carefully cuts everything up and moves the food around until it's just perfect, forget it. He's a dud. The one who digs in and goes for it and relishes it and eats like it's his first and last meal is going to be gangbusters in the sack.

The next time I see Chris I'll ask for her prediction on men who don't bother with a knife or fork and just put their heads down on the plate and inhale.

Intimate Acts

"Emotional intimacy" is a term that comes up frequently when I'm doing focus groups with women or TV shows with active audience participation. At first, I thought it was one of those psychobabble phrases that go in and out of fashion. But after hearing those words—*emotional intimacy*—again and again, I began to realize that there was more to them than trendy jargon.

One of the things that men and women have in common is the absolute need to be loved and to love in return. Emotional intimacy, a joining together of the spirit rather than the flesh, is how this love is conceived. Every human being depends on this process, and it isn't a process at all—that makes it sound too mechanical; there's too much chemistry and magic involved. Anyway, every human being depends on a certain amount of emotional intimacy to maintain balance and happiness and just to survive from day to day.

Where men differ from women is in their ability to have sexual intimacy without emotional intimacy. The link be-

tween the two is not as important for many men. It may
be desirable for them to have emotional intimacy with their
lovers, and it may mean a more satisfying sexual experience, but if it's absent, that's okay too.

Sure, there are women who could care less about emotional intimacy; sex is what's important to them. And there
are men who demand emotional intimacy before they'll
even think about loosening their neckties. There are no
hard-and-fast rules that apply to everyone. But most men
tend to give emotional intimacy a lower priority.

This can become a natural source of conflict between
men and women. When a woman's need for emotional
intimacy is not fulfilled, either before or after sexual intimacy, frustration and disappointment can set in. "What's
wrong with him?" or "What's wrong with me?" are the
kinds of questions that bubble to the surface. And in reality, there is nothing wrong with either of them.

Men move toward emotional intimacy at a slower pace
than women do. They'll probably get there, but it's not
going to be a record-breaking fifty-yard dash. During one
of my *Today* show assignments I had coffee with Cliff, a
long-haul trucker from Illinois. Cliff was complaining
about how women are "in such a damned hurry, all the
time." He said that he'll be dating a woman for the first
time, and everything's going along just fine; suddenly,
she'll be making plans for them as a couple—"We'll go
here . . . we'll go there . . . we'll do this . . ." These two
people—little better than strangers, really—are suddenly
a couple. She sees a permanent relationship forming long
before he does. They're moving down the road to emotional intimacy at very different rates.

A first date is not grounds for rushing out to the mall
and registering your china pattern. Slow down. I'm not
talking about playing hard to get, though; that's a throw-

back to another era. I believe in being reasonably honest and up front about your feelings. Men aren't scared off by straight talk, but they do get nervous when control seems to be slipping away. Finding that you are already coupled before the popcorn gets cold and while the film's opening credits are still rolling comes as a shocker.

Unfortunately, there is no reliable formula for turning on the valve and letting emotional intimacy flow. Certainly, the first date is too early. Look for signs that his need for emotional intimacy is beginning to ignite (don't confuse it with his need for sexual intimacy—that's already burning).

In the Slow Lane of the Fast Track

Lisa and Tom met one New Year's Eve. Before the clock struck twelve they were talking about marriage, and seven days later they were engaged. It was love at first sight, but it didn't last. They are divorced, and I think it's because they were in such a damned hurry. The emotional intimacy that should have developed between them never did. The headlong rush to the altar got in the way. Perversely, by moving so far so fast, Tom leap-frogged over emotional intimacy and went directly to sexual intimacy and the business of marriage. A vital ingredient was always missing from their relationship.

I don't have hard evidence to support my views, but I wouldn't be surprised if I found out that Lisa had projected her own need for emotional intimacy onto Tom. It is easy to use others as a mirror that reflects our own hopes, needs, and standards. It's a great disappointment when a totally different person emerges than the one we've imagined.

I was once asked if there is a way for women to "make" a man more interested in emotional intimacy. As I said at the time, and say again here, it can't be done. Don't try it. He must come to emotional intimacy on his own terms. You can do your best by being your best—just be you. It sounds trite, but it's the only approach that works long-term. Emotional intimacy takes place when there is an honest bond between a man and a woman.

Traveling Men

The vacation-date is getting to be more common these days, but if you're planning to go on a trip with a man, make sure the relationship is on a good, solid, and friendly basis. An African photo safari, a cabin in the woods of Maine, or a quiet beach in the Caribbean are lousy places to discover that your traveling companion is not your kind of guy.

A long weekend can be longer than you think when it is spent with a stranger who turns out to be really strange. A week or two can seem like years. Unlike a date, a vacation requires that you spend twenty-four hours a day together. If the vibes aren't right, April in Paris will feel like February in Juneau.

And no matter whether the invitation involves the Jardin des Tuileries or tundra, it is important to remember that a man is planning on sleeping with his female traveling companion. It is one of the key elements in the equation. Men assume—and often they're wrong—that women understand that passion is also on the itinerary. This can prove to be a source of great embarrassment and consternation, and no amount of hoping that he will do the "right thing" by reserving a separate room or staying on his side of the double bed will salvage the situation. If you don't feel that you know him well enough to come right out and ask if he expects the two of you to be intimate, you probably don't know him well enough to spend a vacation together, with or without sex.

It's not a bad idea to take a few short trips before trying anything with a duration of more than three days. I know a fellow who wouldn't dream of investing in an expensive vacation trip until he has spent at least one "lost weekend" with a new lover. Running from dinner Friday to breakfast Monday, the lost weekend is a marathon of togetherness: lovemaking, soaks in the hot tub, lovemaking, gourmet meals, lovemaking, reading, lovemaking. The idea is to lock the door and say, "To hell with the rest of the world." By Monday morning he knows if they are reasonably compatible.

People change when they are thrown together for long periods of time. Little habits that go unnoticed in the course of an evening can explode into major irritations. By leading up to a long vacation with some short getaways, you'll not only avoid some unpleasant surprises but a comfortable routine will develop. You'll learn each other's likes and dislikes, strengths and weaknesses.

Even this kind of careful advance work is no guarantee of success, though. Before I was married, I had a disastrous vacation in Spain and Portugal with a woman I had known for years. It turned out that we just couldn't travel together for any longer than a few days. By the time we got to Lisbon, the relationship was shot.

Another example: Tanya, who has a close platonic friendship with a man, drew up a written agreement before they traveled together. One clause was that there would never be any crankiness. At the first sign of a mood change, the would-be grouch would have to walk away and cool off. The agreement also included financial arrangements, the itinerary, limits on museum time (Tanya overdoses on more than four hours of culture a day), and built-in solo excursions to give the couple a vacation from each other.

While platonic friends may want to share a room to save money, it is not wise to share a bed. Even the best of intentions can be swept away in a few moments of drowsy passion.

Beware of cruise ships and self-contained resorts. Aside from lowering a lifeboat or hacking your way through the surrounding rain forest, there are no escape routes. You're stuck for the duration if he drops his Prince Charming disguise and turns out to be the frog. Nobody wants to terminate a vacation, but it could be necessary if you wind up with a companion who is emotionally unstable, abuses drugs or alcohol, or indulges in sexual practices that make you uncomfortable.

Split the cost of a vacation fifty-fifty. There's nothing wrong with working a deal around the business mileage you've accumulated through one of the airline frequent-flyer programs. If you take care of the transportation, he can get the hotels. But, as a rule, the formula should come out even on both sides.

If he insists on bankrolling a romantic Roman holiday, you can either sit back and enjoy the Campari and sodas or stay home. There is no escaping the old saw "He who pays the piper calls the tune." You lose a measure of control by being put in the role of honored guest. And that may not be any big worry. However, you should realize that the balance of power is tipped toward the one who is signing the tabs. Paying half gives you a sense of independence. A woman can say, "Hey, I've got a stake in this thing too. I'm not just a puppet. You're not calling all the shots."

I realize that going dutch isn't fashionable these days, but it does offer some practical advantages. For one thing, there are no IOUs involved. Men tend to think that they are buying a sexual lottery ticket when they pay for dinner and drinks. Splitting the cost is a way to signal him that you're not ready to be the grand prize.

If there is no romantic attachment between traveling companions, the normal everyday courtesy of friends keeps the wheels turning smoothly. Nora, an accountant from Cleveland, took several trips with Jeffrey, her piano teacher. He was about fifteen years older than she was and there was no interest in a sexual relationship on either side. They just had a good time together. On a trip to Yugoslavia, Nora met a man who really turned her on. In Dubrovnik, she made up a rather lame excuse and dumped Jeffrey to go off with Hugh. She wrecked the balance of Jeffrey's vacation, and now, looking back on her decision, Nora feels rotten about it. Hugh was in and out of her life in a matter of months. Jeffrey was an old friend and deserved better treatment. He said he didn't mind the Dubrovnik business; he still gives her piano lessons, but they've never traveled together since.

Based on Nora's experience, I would say that it is not a good idea to play musical traveling companions. Exchange telephone numbers and addresses; follow up later, or include your old friend and your new friend in the vacation activities.

Occasionally, worst-case scenarios do happen. If you have to bail out of a vacation, if he is making you miserable, ruining a once-in-a-lifetime experience, then go ahead. You may have to reimburse your former companion for any penalty charges, but it's a small price to pay to salvage your sanity.

And occasionally, best-case scenarios happen. He may be the ideal traveling companion. If he is, bear in mind that while vacations are a good guide to what a guy is like over the long haul, a trip is an unnatural situation. He is out of his native habitat, away from the office and his friends. When this mellow, fun-loving man gets home and back to the job, he could revert to his workaholic routine. But men are rarely able to switch it on and off like that, and you will probably see signs that the beachcomber is yearning to trade in his sandals for the wing-tip shoes.

Knowing What You Want in a Man

"All the guys out there are either married, gay, or idiots." How many times have you heard that lament? I'll bet it runs a close second to "Have a nice day!" Fortunately, it's not true.

Believe me, I understand how tough it is for singles. I've heard gruesome stories from terrific women. But keep looking; that special guy is out there.

There are lots of single men at large in this world, men who may not meet your requirements—looks, intelligence, personality, sense of humor, financial status, philosophy, education. You have to mix and match the items to suit yourself. But if men were forced to guess which factor would head a woman's list most often, it would be money, and we act accordingly by playing the role of big spender in an effort to make a good impression in the early stages of a relationship.

It may go back to the IOUs and buying a ticket in the sexual lottery, which I mentioned earlier in this chapter.

Whatever the source, money generates intense anxiety in men. For starters, there's never enough of it, and I don't care if your name is Donald Trump. I've watched guys make complete fools of themselves trying to prove to women that they commute to work in a convoy of armored cars, and then they turn around and wonder why their lovable, warm, intelligent personalities seem to take a backseat to their bank balances.

Anxiety aside, many times it actually is income or professional status or power that qualify or disqualify men from the dating game. Male nurses are a perfect example. I did a story for the *Today* show on men in nontraditional occupations, and the male nurses—guys who you'd think would be working in a bachelor's paradise, given the lopsided male-to-female ratio in hospitals—said it is more hell than heaven. The women, these men contend, are all more interested in the doctors. One of them told me, "Here I am . . . I'm single, heterosexual, not bad-looking—but it's no go. All I get from the nurses is an earful of complaints about what shits the doctors are. And at the end of the day they're climbing into a Mercedes with M.D. license plates."

Okay, revenge is sweet. We all get what we deserve, and perhaps guys who have chased after the perfect "10" deserve to have their checkbooks leered at and fondled. But I'm less concerned about this sort of rough justice than I am about men and women losing out on what might have been solid relationships because the dollar signs obscured the love signs.

Mating ritual seems to require the male of the couple to prove that he's got money to burn. We've been stoking the fire since we were teenagers. It's those ideas and attitudes left over from adolescence that tend to trip us up as adults. Which stereotype came first, Mr. High Roller or

Miss Gold Digger? While there is no way to know for sure, they probably hatched simultaneously out of the same egg, the one that's all over our faces when we refuse to grow up and look at other people as people, not objects—sex objects or success objects.

If good men are hard to find, rich good men are even harder to find. The search restricts women to a small pool of available men whose life-style and values may be at odds with a capacity for loving, sharing, and commitment.

Examine your priorities and find out what you want in a man. Is he a grown-up version of the little big spender? Or is he a mature adult whose sum total adds up to more than the parts of his financial portfolio and career profile?

Men Are Men, Not Success Objects

The classic Hollywood couple, it has always seemed to me, is one of those sixty-five-year-old studio heads—bald, pot-bellied, sagging jowls—with a gorgeous twenty-two-year-old blonde on his arm. What's going on? They've met each other's needs.

She is his sexual fantasy and fulfills his requirements for sexual reinforcement of his ego, those things we talked about in Chapter Four. He is her "sugar daddy," with more than enough money to compensate for the wrinkles and the paunch. It's no matter that he is positively ugly and probably boorish. The money, the power, and the status meet her needs.

She is a sex object and he is a success object.

The mogul and his lady friend know what they're doing. Or they think they know. Hollywood manufactures illusions, but the rest of us have to be careful that we don't fool ourselves into believing that our motives are always pure. He just wants me for my body and she just wants me for my checkbook are two sides to the same counterfeit coin. Flip it, and men and women both lose.

His money could be gone with the next box-office flop and her looks may fade. Then neither of them would get any dividends from a deal that seemed so simple, so practical, at the beginning, but turned out to be cold and empty in the end.

The Ms. and the Misogynist

About once a year I have dinner with Susan. If we met on a more frequent basis, I'm afraid the friendship wouldn't last. Susan is a free-lance graphic designer, and she is very good at it. But I'm convinced that her career has been hurt by Susan's favorite topic—abominable men. Snowmen, showmen, all men, it doesn't make any difference. She spends hours bad-mouthing the lot.

"All New York men," she is fond of declaring, "are married, gay, or screwed up in the head." (A standard variation on the "married, gay, or idiots" putdown I mentioned a few pages back.)

"Look at my chin, Susan," I said to her one time. "I shaved this morning, but it's late in the day. See, facial hair. Take my word for it, I'm a man."

"You're married."

"I wasn't born married," I said. "So, then, I'm gay or screwed up, I suppose?"

"Bob, you're different."

If we had been making small talk—discussing the weather, grumbling about the irritating quirks of dates and mates—there'd be no problem. But what Susan doesn't realize is that she has built a barrier between herself and

men. I'm an old friend—and "different" (so she says)—
yet, I'm very careful about what I say and do around
her. At any moment my parole could be revoked and
I'd be doing time at a maximum-security prison for male
monsters. It hardly creates an atmosphere of trust and
intimacy.

As for dating, Susan spends a lot of time going alone
to films at the Museum of Modern Art. And her social
contacts with women who have reasonably rewarding relationships with men seem strained and fitful.

For Susan, the negative feelings toward men have become an overwhelming obstacle to friendship, love, and
enduring relationships.

Misogynists—men who hate women—are caught in
the same bind. They end up becoming social cripples. Normal interaction between the two sexes is difficult, painful,
and sometimes impossible.

Most often, the hostility is not at all subtle. You won't
have to ask yourself, "Is this guy a woman hater?" You'll
know. And when you know, don't try to reform him. It's
a job for a skilled psychotherapist. There's no way that
one last temper tantrum or diatribe against women—
against you—will get it out of his system.

CHAPTER NINE

BALD SPOTS

Question: Why do men leave their dirty socks on the floor expecting somebody else—the women in their lives —to pick them up?

Answer: I suspect this question comes from the woman in my life. First, the flip answer—do we look stupid? Those things stink. Now, to be serious, I think men want to be mothered sometimes. It's similar to the instinct that women have to be fathered. Every time a guy holds a door open for a woman, it is a reminder of the big strong dad who took care of her. Most men are conditioned to be doers, strivers, and initiators, but, occasionally, we like to be taken care of too. The problem is that many men aren't very good at asking for the take-care-of-me treatment, and in an indirect way we do it by leaving our socks around.

One of the advantages of living with a guy before marriage is that you can find out how much "mothering" he needs. A genuine slob, or someone who believes picking up socks is woman's work, can be edited out of your life before it's too late.

"Take care of me" is the why, and I guess you probably would like to know the what—what to do about it. I think men need their own territory and their own space. If it is physically and financially possible, give him his own bathroom. A space in the basement for his tools and a work area is a good idea. Readers or tinkerers appreciate a place to do their things. Men need a sense of territory, even if it's only a garage.

Tell him he can be sloppy in his own private lair, but in the bedroom neatness counts. Kid him, cajole him, but don't beat him over the head about it. Praise—a little positive reinforcement whenever the socks wind up in the hamper—will help you move toward the day when he will become a fully certified neatnik.

Question: Why do men go crazy over a receding hairline?

Answer: Doctor Joy Browne, the psychologist, broadcaster, and author of *Nobody's Perfect: Good Advice for Blame-Free Living,* says hair is to men what breasts are to women: a symbol of self-esteem and sexuality, and a source of appeal to the opposite sex. A man does feel that there is a loss of power and virility when he is losing his hair. Maybe it goes back to Samson and Delilah. In our society we don't give bonus points to bald men.

There are a few exceptions. A neighbor who had been doing one of those comb-over numbers with his hair to cover a balding spot—you make one lock of hair stretch from Cleveland to Carson City—decided after seeing Sean Connery appear without his "rug" that it was okay to display the bald truth. There's no sexier, more virile man in the world than Sean Connery, or at least the characters Connery plays. James Bond is James Bond, even though at the time the films were shot, Connery was wearing a toupee.

Never tease a man about losing his hair—never. You

could diplomatically suggest hair transplants or one of the other processes for restoring hair. Better yet, make him feel comfortable about his hair and let him know that you will still love him with or without it. Help him to accept himself.

Question: Why do men leave the toilet seat up?
Answer: Why do women leave the toilet seat down?

CHAPTER TEN

TEASERS AND FLIRTS

Men have a low sexual boiling point. I'd say it's somewhere in the vicinity of 33 degrees Fahrenheit. Give us a few seconds to chip the ice off our jockey shorts and look out.

This is probably why mothers have traditionally warned their daughters that "nice girls don't flirt." But, of course, nice girls do flirt, and I hope they always will.

Now, having just come out foursquare in favor of flirtatiousness, I had better issue something on the order of the surgeon general's warning displayed on cigarette packs.

Warning: Flirtations have been known to lead to misunderstandings, embarrassment, and anger. Damage to careers could result. Marriages can be jeopardized. In some cases, physical harm can occur.

Flirting and Hurting

Flirt. Some words, and this is one of them, pack their meaning into the sound. Say "flirt," and you hear—bubbly, sexy, playful.

But there is another word, a term, actually, that men use to describe the ugly side of the flirt: "cockteaser."

Again, the meaning is in the sound. You won't hear the pain, the anger, and the violence in any euphemism. It may shock and offend some women to see the word *cockteaser* on this page, but I'm using it to make an important point.

The state of temporary insanity that overtakes men when they're sexually aroused always makes them easy prey to the woman who is a hater, not a lover. Women who lead men to think that an encounter is headed for bed and hours of torrid ecstasy and who then end the evening with a handshake make them so angry that they return hostility with hostility.

I think that most of the time these women know what they're doing; it may be subconscious in some cases, but the hostility is there nonetheless. And I'm not talking about "misunderstandings." Most men and women can remember times when they got their signals crossed. Everyone gets a few free "whoops!" cards. It's living dangerously, deliberately arousing a man and then walking away, for whatever motive—revenge, power trips, cheap thrills. It's like pulling the pin on a hand grenade. The explosion may not take place in your apartment; I know a guy who broke his hand by smashing it into a closed elevator door after leaving a lady who had suddenly gone from fire to ice. The grenade could go off months or years later, and it may destroy silently, ripping apart a relationship that seemed permanent and solid.

The Granny Gambit

Flirtation is not the problem. Flirtation is fine. It gets the juices flowing, the adrenaline pumping, and the sparks flying.

But you know the difference between flirtation and cockteasing. Don't start telling bedtime stories unless you mean to get into bed. Men have their own hostile version of this game. I call it relationship teasing.

Men are well aware that women are equally vulnerable when it comes to the need for a loving relationship. Relationship teasing can explain the guy who on the first date is saying, "Oh, I want you to meet my family . . . get to know my best friend, Joe . . . there's a favorite spot I want you to see." And it triggers visions of a rich and wonderful relationship when his only objective is seduction.

Relationship teasing is as hostile an act as cockteasing. The sting comes the next morning when he's gone before breakfast and never bothers to call again.

Be wary when things start moving too fast too soon. If he has telescoped six months of relationship foreplay down into six minutes of heavy breathing about Thanksgiving at Grandma's farm, he may be figuring that you're the turkey. Watch out for relationship teasers. Put the brakes on if it does not seem to be the logical time for that kind of talk.

And don't be a cockteaser; an otherwise pleasant evening will end unpleasantly. If he leaves frustrated, you have probably seen the last of him. If he returns, there will be a lot of anger and resentment under the surface. Somehow, I don't think that's what you are looking for in a man.

Come On Without Coming On

First dates are difficult for everyone. Spending several hours alone with a stranger challenges one's social skills. And there is always sexual tension. The classic ques-

tions—"Will she, or won't she?" "Will he, or won't he?" —
are rumbling like distant thunder on a summer evening.

Am I saying that all men are overtly, consciously cal-
culating their chances of getting their dates into bed from
the moment the doorbell rings? No, it's not quite so raw
as all that. But as I've noted before, the sexual component
of a man's relationship with a woman has a powerful influence. From the beginning, he is looking for landmarks
and road signs that will tell him where he is headed.

Posting the highway is a dicey business. I've asked men
how they know whether they are looking at a STOP sign
or a YIELD sign. Leonard's answer was probably the most
romantic and the least revealing. He said, "I can see it
in her eyes." I pressed him to explain. "If the evening is
going well, you'll get good eye contact. She'll probably
start off nervous. . . . I know I do. The eye contact will be
very brief and skittish. As things warm up, the eyes will
start to settle down. If, after a while, the conversation
turns intimate or suggestive and the eyes are steady, I
know . . ."

"Know what?"

"I just know," he said.

Thanks, Len, you're a big help.

Second Sight

Actually, you may gain valuable insight—and I don't intend that as a pun—from Leonard's eye theory. Eyes are
very revealing. A poker player who can read his oppo-
nents' eyes is hard to beat. He can see glimmers of anxiety,
delight, and uncertainty. I've heard so much about shifty-
eyed liars that somebody with a strange story and a steady
gaze is the one who worries me.

The power of our eyes to communicate what's going on in our heads shouldn't be underestimated. If you are interested in a man, let your eyes do the talking. It may help to avoid crossing the line between flirting and teasing.

Foreplay and Foul Play

In one of my discussion groups, Bill told us that he believes women have tried to encourage him to follow up on a first date by a farewell round of heavy petting. They don't intend to have sexual intercourse, but the foreplay is intense, too intense to be suddenly cut off. The message— "I'm interested"—gets garbled by the frustration. Flirtation has turned into cockteasing.

Bill's observation prompted another member of the group to say that he had brought a woman home from a first date after an enjoyable and chaste evening and stood on the doorstep wondering what to do next when she gave him a good-night kiss that included a lot of tongue (hers). After the embrace, she turned and went into the house. He got the message, and called her for a second date the next morning. The relationship lasted for several years.

Flirting in the Office

A little goes a long way. And again, it's men who spoil the fun. The book of professional etiquette was written long before women joined men in the workplace as colleagues and supervisors. We are still learning the new do's and don'ts.

When I listen to men discuss their female associates, I get the impression that they swing from extreme to extreme. On one hand they underestimate women; women are newcomers and novices and not much of a threat. On the other hand, women are seen as potentially deadly rivals who can pull all sorts of unfair tricks. They wear makeup, designer clothes, and eye-catching jewelry. They laugh at the boss's bad jokes and get return telephone calls from notoriously uncommunicative customers.

Judicious flirting is a useful career tool. It can help women to compensate for the handicap of not being "one of the boys" swapping jock talk about the big game. But the key word is *judicious*.

And here are three other rules; let's call them Berk's Laws of Flirtation:

1. Only flirt in a public place.
2. Play no favorites. Flirt, at least a little, with every guy in the office.
3. Perfect your blush. A man who "misunderstands" understands when he sees a red face.

Clothes Encounters

Dressing with feminine flair is another form of flirtatiousness. But avoid miniskirts at work unless you work in a cocktail lounge. Appropriate dress is of great importance, and men will not take you seriously in the office if you're wearing plunging necklines and low backs or hemlines that are way above the knee. It doesn't mean that everything has got to be gray and pinstriped. Go for color and style, but make it fit the occasion (men are learning the color-and-style lesson, and they've picked up more than a few pointers from women).

Still, men tend to be fashion illiterates when it comes

to women's clothing. They know what they like and what they don't like. Two-piece skirt-and-jacket numbers, inspired by boring traditional men's business uniforms, make women look like Lee Iacocca in drag.

I recently read a newspaper article by a woman lawyer who objects whenever a group of men and women are referred to as "you guys." She pointed out that women are not "guys." Okay, but the counselor might want to check her clothes closet to see whether her semantic sensitivity is consistent with her sartorial inclinations.

CHAPTER ELEVEN

BOYS JUST WANT TO HAVE SEX

As your "spy," I've got to tell you that sex is on the front burner for virtually every man you will ever meet in your life. It's just the way things are.

I know, I know. You're thinking, *Typical man—after one chapter on dating and a little flirting, he's talking about sex.*

Chapter Twelve deals with the subject of commitment. So readers might prefer to skip ahead and then come back here. In the ideal world, sex should follow commitment. But in the real world, it often doesn't work that way. Since this is a book about men, sex has rudely elbowed its way in front of commitment.

First of all, guys will do and say just about anything to get women into bed. We can't help it. The issue has nothing to do with respect, love, or commitment.

If you say to a man early in the relationship, even on the first date, "I need a spiritual, loving relationship before I can give my body to a man, before I can engage in the most intimate of acts," he will agree with you. One spiritual, loving relationship coming right up. He will tell you what you want to hear. Men are goal-oriented, in addition to having the hots 99 percent of the time, and that means getting the lovely creature who is sitting on the other side of the table into the sack tonight, tomorrow night, the sooner the better.

I recently asked a group of guys if they agreed with this proposition, and all but one said that I was right on the money. The dissenter felt that sex complicates a relationship, and he prefers to avoid complications until the relationship is firmly established. I tried him a second time with a what-if comeback: What if he knew that the sex would be purely physical and would not create an emotional undertow to complicate the still tentative relationship? Immediately, Gary, a stock-market analyst, said in that case he would be analyzing the most direct route between the lady's living-room couch and her king-size bed.

This group was particularly interesting because one of its members was gay, and he contended that homosexual men have very masculine tendencies. He wasn't kidding. Like all men, they want to have sex. Social or relationship foreplay—I guess the old-fashioned term is "courtship"— is very often of secondary importance.

By recognizing that a man is following a different agenda, and there's that word *different* again, you may be better able to understand what's going on when he suggests that breakfast in bed is his favorite meal of the day —even though the two of you are only just starting on your first round of beers.

He is not saying that you are "easy," or that he intends to settle down for life. What he is saying, and you can forget the words entirely, is pretty damned primitive and closely akin to the mating call of a bull moose.

Now, suppose you respond to the call of the wild. Does that mean he won't respect you in the morning? Or that he does not want a relationship to grow out of the encounter? Absolutely not. He may very well want to have

a long-term relationship with you. Men are not immune
to the emotional power that is generated by sexual intimacy. Their priorities, however—lust first, love later—
can't be overlooked.

There are couples who make love on the first date and
end up spending a lifetime together. Others wait a while
and get the same results. I think too much is made of the
"Do we or don't we?" question (and the "When do we do
the doing?" question). And I'm certainly in no position to
generalize with hard-and-fast answers. It's an individual
decision all the way.

I had an amusing dinner party recently with two friends
who couldn't get their bedtimes straight. He swore that
they nearly brought the waterbed to a boil on the first
night; she insisted that the romance didn't heat up quite
that fast. They couldn't be happier together. It simply
makes no difference to them whether the earth moved on
the first date or the fifth.

A man's interest in sex isn't devoid of emotion and
responsibility. Sure, there are some who say "I'm going
to score, and when I do, it's good-bye, baby." Sex to them
is just another form of basketball. But there is more to
physical love than a good slam dunk, and most men have
the capacity and the desire to be lovers in the best sense
of the word.

But . . . but . . . but if he doesn't call you soon after
that torrid first date (preferably the next day), it's a good
reason to write him off. There aren't many plausible excuses to justify a man not calling you under those circumstances. "I was thrown in jail . . . rushed to the
hospital . . . sent to Patagonia on business" may hold
water. Otherwise, he is just being rude and unfeeling. The
chances of a healthy relationship forming after that kind
of a gaffe are extremely remote. He may call again, es-

pecially when the sexual sap is rising, and you may actually want to see him. A friendly arm's-length lunch is safer, unless you have a thing for being hurt.

Sticking to Your Agenda

Having sex in the early stages of a relationship will not necessarily stunt its growth; nor is it a guarantee that something, anything, will come of the affair.

Sex is spelled s-e-x, not i-o-u. A man does not feel indebted after he gets out of bed. So, then, what does a woman do? Does she, or doesn't she? The answer will grow out of the knowledge that he has his agenda and you have your agenda. Stick to your agenda. If you want to know more about him, more about the way the two of you interact, before becoming sexually intimate—then make that clear to him and don't back down. He will do it your way if he is really interested in you.

One way to avoid awkwardness is to control the romantic venue. After an evening out, an invitation back to your place is liable to be read as the prelude to a more passionate encounter. To avoid a wrestling match, suggest that the cozy bar around the corner would be the perfect place for the last drink of the evening. Choosing a semi-public place for a farewell embrace is another effective tactic for letting a man know that you're interested but intend to set your own pace.

If a man cares about you and a potential relationship, he will postpone the immediate gratification of his sexual needs. But you've got to be careful about sending mixed signals (and serving him a cognac while he is sitting ten feet from your open bedroom door is definitely a mixed signal); eventually you may have to spell it out and make your objective absolutely clear. Otherwise, his passion will be the deciding factor. If you say, "No, not tonight," and explain why, he will wait. If he won't, and his sexual agenda is paramount, then you are probably better off watching the late movie alone.

But keep in mind that this is not an open-ended deal. His need for sexual fulfillment is an integral aspect of an intimate relationship between a man and a woman. You can't postpone it forever and expect a man to develop a taste for celibacy. He isn't built that way. And just as sex is not an IOU chit, it is also not a reward for good behavior. Relationships work when they are win-win situations, to use a phrase that's slipped into our vocabulary in the last few years. Not you win and he loses; not you lose and he wins. Both of you win because both agendas have been met. The items on those agendas are matters of personal choice, value judgments. But to provide a basic example, let's say that he rates good sex high on the list, while for you, good friendship is a priority. The win-win comes when there is enough care, compromise, and mutual consideration to make it possible for both of you to get what you need. In the process, a melding of agendas takes place: The sex is better, the friendship stronger.

Sex Does Strange Things to His Brain

When you throw the switch and the sexual circuits start to smoke, men are so turned on they lose their equilibrium. I'm not exaggerating, and I wonder if women realize that men aren't pretending to be nuts; they do go a little goofy—make that a lot goofy—when it comes to sex.

When all the fuses are about to blow, somebody has got to be semisensible. And that somebody is you, because it's not going to be him.

I know this is not a very satisfactory notion in many ways. There seems to be the implication that we are stuck with the stereotypes of the hot, sex-crazed male and the cool, prudent female. Some men have been too quick to excuse themselves and others with "Oh, forget it . . . Bill just got carried away. He can't keep his hands off anything in a skirt." Worse, far worse: "It was her fault. She asked for it."

Nonsense. Men know right from wrong, whether they are lying in bed or sitting on the board of directors. Yet this nonsense testifies to the disorienting power of the sexual urge. It can draw us across the boundary lines between courtesy and discourtesy, civility and incivility, morality and immorality.

Honest men start telling white lies when it comes to sex. They lie to you because they lie to themselves. The best explanation for what's going on isn't really an explanation at all, it's an earthy Yiddish proverb: "When the cock gets hard, the brains get soft."

Men will throw away a fortune. They will spend outrageous sums of money on a date because they think it will help them get a woman into bed. But they lose the power to make rational judgments when things start happening south of their belt buckles.

I once worked with a guy who loathes cigarette smoke. It's almost pathological. He gets nauseated, headaches; he's a wreck if anybody lights up—anybody, that is, except a woman he is anxious to get into the sack with. And he tells the story on himself. Things will be progressing nicely, a fine dinner, a bottle of wine, and then the lady asks if he minds if she smokes. "Oh, no," my friend says.

"I don't mind. Go right ahead." He doesn't want anything
negative introduced into the evening until after he has
achieved his objective. And these aren't one-night stands,
either. But the next time they are together, he will let it
drop that her smoking is a problem.

Dishonest? Yes. Warped? Absolutely. Lust overrides
the genuine physical repulsion he feels for cigarette smoke.

Luis put a personal ad in his local newspaper hoping
to meet interesting women. He described himself in the
ad as a feminist. Now, this guy is as much a feminist as
Ronald Reagan is a socialist—he's just not.

I asked him, "What are you trying to do? If you're a
feminist, pal, then Sonny Liston was a prima ballerina."
And I knew what the answer would be before I asked the
question.

"That's what women want to hear," he said. If you
need a translation: Sure, it's an outrageous lie, but it will
do wonders for my sex life.

It did, too. The ad drew a heavy response from accomplished and attractive women. Luis got what he was after,
which, incidentally, wasn't only sex. I said, "wasn't *only*
sex"; he had a healthy interest in the things of the flesh.
But Luis also wanted to know some of the best and bright-
est women the city had to offer, women who were making
things happen in business, finance, law, communications.
Luis wanted stimulation—sexual, intellectual, and social.
"I am not a feminist," or words to that effect, probably
would not have helped Luis sell himself to these women.
Probably.

Luis was being a hypocrite, as many men are when
they hoist the flag of feminism. He—they—sail under false
colors to avoid being blown out of the water. As a serious
crime it rates somewhere between jaywalking and ripping
the government tag off a mattress. "I am a feminist" is

another way to say "I am not Archie Bunker," a know-nothing cretin camped out in front of the TV bellowing at the little woman to get another bowl of potato chips. It's a form of social shorthand, like a pair of suspenders or jogging shoes with an Alcott & Andrews pinstriped frock.

So, when you hear the words "I am a feminist," he may be the brave new man envisioned by feminists a quarter of a century ago, or he may be good old Luis.

Ploys and Plays

Nearly every sexually active man has his own seduction strategy. It has evolved since the day he first lost his virginity. The ploys that work are refined to be used again, and those that don't are dropped from the repertoire. A college classmate I haven't seen for years is probably still whining and begging his way into bed. He had no shame, and since it got him what he was after, there is every chance he will be pulling the same stunts until the day they wheel him away to the nursing home.

A seduction strategy that relies on coercion or force, however, isn't a strategy, and it isn't seduction. Forced sex is rape.

Most men know the difference, even though they may persist after a woman has let it be known that she is not interested in a demonstration of the latest Tantrik massage technique. As I said earlier, he wants to get you into bed—the sooner the better. But you control the timing.

Brad forgot this fact of life when he tried to browbeat Annie into having sex. It wasn't that they hadn't been intimate; the relationship was well established. But Annie was facing a busy day at work and she wanted to head back to her apartment rather than into Brad's bedroom.

They had been kissing and fondling each other on the couch, and when Brad suggested that he wanted to make love to her, Annie told him about her plans to make it an early night. Brad was hot, and he was ready to take his passion through the express lane (eight items or less), if necessary. He said that she didn't have to spend the night. Annie still wasn't interested.

At that point Brad went too far. Let's call it the you-owe-it-to-me routine. He said, "I'm a considerate lover, a thoughtful lover, I always wait until you come. Isn't that true?" Annie agreed: He was a thoughtful lover. "Then, I want you to do something for me now," Brad insisted.

Annie stood her ground, but not without tears and an unpleasant end to the evening. She loved him and under other circumstances would have gladly jumped into the sack. I suspect that Brad learned a lesson. "You owe it to me" didn't work; in fact, it wrecked the evening. His seduction strategy has been revised. A few days later, the couple did make love and it was particularly ardent and satisfying. Maybe she was trying a little harder; maybe he was trying a little harder. Either way, it worked out for both of them.

The Annie and Brad story is consistent with my theory that there isn't any such thing as seduction. It's too easy to claim that "he seduced me," or that "she led me astray." Sexual intercourse between consenting adults doesn't happen until we decide to make it happen. Annie decided it wasn't going to happen.

Even so, Annie made a serious mistake. Knowing her man and the business pressure she was facing, Brad's couch was the wrong place to be at the wrong time. Dinner at a restaurant, a movie, or a stroll along the waterfront would have been a better idea.

Some men say they resent being put in awkward positions that almost require them to make a pass at a woman. Require? Clearly, Brad was doing the requiring. But recent surveys indicate that a high percentage of the men questioned claim that they have been coerced into having sex. Although I suspect that many women are justifiably skeptical about claims like that, it is valuable to know that such feelings exist. Seen from that new perspective, the old stereotypes—Man the Seducer, Woman the Seduced—begin to crumble. In their place we have sex as a fifty-fifty proposition.

Eye-Jobs

I'm more than halfway through a chapter on sex and the word *penis* hasn't been used once—that must be a record of some kind. But since I've now used it, I can talk freely about a man's number-one erogenous zone—his eyes.

We are visual animals. Touch, smell, hearing, rational thinking, all take a backseat to the visual. And this is not a subtle characteristic by any means. There is a lot he doesn't notice, but the things he can't miss, he can't miss. To heat up a relationship, buy sexy, erotic negligees and underwear. He will, I guarantee, pay attention. Play to his optic nerves.

If you fear that this will reduce you to a sex object, look at it this way: When a couple is making love, both partners are functioning as sex objects. It is the way we get turned on. Outside the bedroom, the stimulation is intellectual, professional, or from whatever other source is appropriate to the circumstances. There is an interaction among all the stimulants that gives the best relationships energy and excitement.

Many of us are self-conscious and inhibited about our

sexuality. The Victorian era ghosts still tell us that there is something wrong with giving and receiving pleasure with our bodies. Denying the visual side of lovemaking is a way to placate those ghosts and convince them that sexuality hasn't been allowed to get the upper hand.

One of the differences between men and women is the reaction to pornography, and I use the term in its most general and blandest sense. As I said, men tend to go for visual stimulation, including pictures. I've often wondered if the birthrate goes up nine months after *Sports Illustrated*'s annual swimsuit issue hits the magazine racks. On the other hand, the market for "bodice rippers," as romance and Gothic novels are referred to in publishing, tends to be female. The text and its effect on the imagination is what stimulates women. For the most part, pornographic books have to be awfully raw to get the same response out of men. They cross the sexual fantasy threshold by a different route.

I took part in a TV show that featured a lingerie fashion show. Every guy in the audience was up; there was no doubt about it. The models were not professionals. Instead, the producers asked housewives and women from nearby offices to come in and wear this really sexy stuff. It wasn't a beauty contest, with a parade of Miss America – class perfect bodies, but the men were all eyes, believe me (mine are still bulging, as it so happens).

To drive the point home, the show also included a woman who teaches the art of striptease, and her students are average women with no plans to start careers on the bump-and-grind circuit. They intend their performances for "his" eyes only. Moreover, there was a photographer there who does what she calls boudoir shots for women to give to the men in their lives. Her customers pose in their sexiest underwear and nightgowns. One of them even brought in an old flannel number because it was her husband's favorite.

The eyes have it.

A Gun in His Pocket

Sandra is a very savvy lady. She has been around a lot of guys, so when she asked me this particular question it did catch my attention. "Why," she wanted to know, "are guys hung up about the size of their cocks?" I could clean it up and use a more clinical term for the male reproductive organ, but Sandra doesn't talk that way (and I think the same goes for most people these days).

I couldn't supply an answer right off, but I did start to do a little research. Unscientific research, to be sure. I've got a few good women friends who aren't easily daunted, and they weren't offended when I passed along Sandra's query. They all said that she was right about the fact that many men are anxious about their penis size.

Okay. Premise sort of confirmed. But why? I know this is the age of anxiety, but there are more important things to worry about. My panel of experts gave me the clue I needed. Each said the size of her lover's penis was important to her. And this may be the answer to why men are "hung up." We are aware—without ever asking—that penis size is important to many women. There was a time, and not long ago, when most women did not have the range of sexual experience to allow them to "comparison shop." Today, many women—or, if you believe the statistics, the majority—know the difference between small, medium, and large. And men know that they know.

It probably reflects my skittishness as a male about this issue, but I'm going to be particularly careful to hide the identity of the man in the next example. He is not an architect, and he is not from Santa Fe. Let's just pretend that he is, though.

The fictional architect knows that women know that his penis is, in the words of one former lover, "absolutely minuscule." She told me that he was handsome, charming, intelligent—close to perfection. She was desperate to climb into the sack on their first date. But he didn't make the move right away. When it finally did happen, she was shocked and broke off the relationship. She didn't tell him the real reason, but it was over. This woman said she knew immediately that the relationship would go nowhere. There was no way he could have satisfied her sexually— I'm quoting her on that score and passing it on to you (and yes, there are ways other than intercourse to get sexual satisfaction)—and she broke it off.

Another comparison shopper, Nancy T., told me that she once thought it didn't make a difference. Nancy, though, changed her mind after a romantic vacation in Jamaica with a "well-hung cop," to use her description.

Of course, this is all very subjective. For every Nancy I could probably find a Joan or a Julie to argue that "it's what you do with what you've got" that is important. Studies using far more sophisticated techniques than mine show that penis size is not a factor in a woman's sexual pleasure. I suspect that there are two valid answers to the question of whether the size of a lover's penis is important. One is prim and proper and delivered in an intellectual context. The other, the one I got, is down and dirty, with a direct connection to passion and pleasure. All I can say is that sex therapists report that men frequently come into their offices for treatment after having been rejected by women because their cocks were too small.

This penis-size business is not something that men just

made up on their own, a male phallic myth. It's apparently a real factor in the sex lives of millions of men and women. It's interesting, really, that women often accuse men of treating them as sex objects, body parts, rather than human beings. Yet some women do exactly the same thing to men. They are just body parts, spare parts, large or small parts.

One of the points that I keep coming back to is the need for men and women to be direct and not hint about important things. In this case, however, being direct is risky. Telling a man that he is too small is like informing an Italian chef that he doesn't use enough garlic. It would be a real assault on his self-esteem. Positive reinforcement in other areas of his sexual performance could inspire him to be a more skillful lover. And ultimately, if you're not satisfied, it may be time to end the relationship.

When Enough's Enough

"It's not over until it's over" and "It's not over until the fat lady sings" are cockeyed truisms that are fun to toss around. But most of the time, knowing when to drop the final curtain on a relationship isn't so easy to recognize.

Here are a few landmarks to look for when the road starts to get rocky:

A pattern of verbal abuse
Physical threats
Physical violence
Flagrant cheating
Repeated irresponsible behavior (e.g., running up huge debts, disappearing for long periods of time, not showing up for dates, failure to keep commitments)

Sexual abstinence that's not related to illness or other readily explainable factors

Bisexuality

A relationship that's built exclusively around his sexual gratification

Ultimatums that involve ending the relationship "unless" you meet certain conditions

Taking an Anatomy Lesson

Until recently, men were faulted for being blissfully ignorant about female anatomy. And we were ignorant. Many of the trappings of our Victorian heritage were stripped away in the 1960s and 1970s, and without all those fig leaves we've been able to grasp the difference—literally and figuratively—between the simple mechanics of coitus and the "zipless fuck," to use Erica Jong's racy term.

The lubricating function performed by foreplay, for instance, is not something that men learn by experiencing their own bodies. We're not built that way, and so we have to be told that women are different. And, thank God, women have told us.

Now it's my turn to tell you. A guy's penis is not a weed to be pulled out of the ground, or the handle of a slot machine for yanking up and down. Go easy.

Masturbation seems like a harsh tug-of-war kind of thing. It isn't. Gentleness and a little lubrication would be welcomed by most men.

Your body has many erotic zones. Men are still learning about a woman's sensual landscape. But our bodies have fewer "buttons" that can be pushed, and the penis has only a small area, underneath its head, where the most sensitive nerve endings are concentrated. That's not to say that everything else is dead; it's just good to know where to find the switch when you want to light up the chandelier.

Heavy Breathing

Life would be a lot easier if I could say flatly that *all* men do this or *all* men do that. My readers would then be guaranteed that for every specific effect there's a matching cause. I said men are simple, not robots!

It's really a matter of probabilities. Men are probably going to be less demanding about establishing a solid relationship before they become sexually intimate with a woman. Probably. But *Men's Health* magazine conducted a survey of its readers that indicated nearly half of men over forty believe that to enjoy sex it is absolutely essential to have the love and affection of their sexual partner. The figure for men under forty was only a few points lower.

If *Men's Health* is on the right track, it means that fewer than 50 percent of the men are orchestrating 100 percent of all "one-night stands." Otherwise, there are a lot of men out there who are having sex and not enjoying it. What I am getting at, aside from teasing the researchers, is to point out that men do have the capacity and the desire to make sexual intercourse more than a few minutes of heavy breathing.

I am never surprised, though, when a guy tells me that, to him, sex is nothing more than the "hunt." And it is not uncommon to hear men use that hunting analogy when they are talking about women. It is important to realize that there are some built-in contradictory impulses at work. A man can switch back and forth between them, demanding sex raw and on the half shell when he is twenty-two, romance and relationships at thirty, and flings with total strangers at forty. Age and experience are factors, but these sea changes can take place over the course of three days or three hours.

The pressure of inner conflicts, such as a desire for total control, an idealized self-image, the need for flattery—conditions addressed by Dr. Karen Horney in a classic study, *Our Inner Conflicts: A Constructive Theory of Neurosis*—can bubble to the surface like underground streams. Changing sexual patterns reflect the ups and down of everyday life.

Hair Triggers

I wish this book had pictures. If it did, Gale would be the centerfold. You should see how beautiful she is. But Gale's beauty is a problem. For one thing, it gets in the way of her sexual fulfillment.

We were at the beach when she began to tell me about Martin, a man in her office who had been slowly easing up to the subject of asking her out on a date. It had taken several weeks, but Martin finally suggested dinner.

"How'd it go?" I asked.

"Not great," she said, frowning as she slathered suntan cream on her legs. I was finding it difficult to breathe as I watched the process. She continued with the story: "We went back to my place and sprinted into the bedroom and . . ."

"And?"

"And he came within three and a half seconds." Gale grimaced as she put the cap back on the plastic bottle. "It happens to me all the damned time!"

I suggested that maybe she was exaggerating a little. "Twelve seconds, then," she said.

Maybe if we had been someplace other than the beach I would have overlooked the obvious. But the obvious was right there in front of me. "Gale," I said, "you're lucky that Martin got his pants off in time. You are such a turn-on it's perfectly understandable that the guy couldn't control himself the first time he climbed into your bed. Give him a second chance. Coming that quickly is a compliment."

Gale assumed that Martin and other men she had been with were in need of a sex therapist to cure them of premature ejaculation. She didn't understand the power of her own sex appeal, and I think that's the same for most women. Couples who expect perfection the first time they have sexual intercourse are usually disappointed. There is too much excitement, fear, and passion for skilled lovemaking.

I know men who say they masturbate before they go out on a first date to make sure they are not too quick on the trigger. Les, a former Secret Service agent, tells a tale on himself about the time he tried to impress a new girlfriend. He smeared his penis with a special cream that was supposed to retard ejaculation. By the time Les reached orgasm, he was nearly ready to faint from exhaustion, and his girlfriend refused to have sexual intercourse again for a month.

If a woman climaxes early, men don't think twice about it (except to applaud themselves for exceptional virility). Men know they must try to postpone ejaculation or else there will be an intermission in the middle of the main feature.

Impotentates

It's probably going overboard to say that all men fear impotence. The older a man gets, the more aware he is of the changes that are taking place in his sexual circuitry. It may take him a lot longer to be aroused than when he was eighteen. Orgasms are less explosive and recovery time between them lengthens. This can be worrisome; anxiety, stress, pressure, all affect sexual performance. Worry about it enough and you've got dejection instead of erection.

A man who suddenly becomes impotent should be encouraged to see his doctor. While psychological factors usually set off the sexual circuit breakers, impotence can be a symptom of a serious illness. Diabetes is one example, and while impotence is not always associated with the condition, it does occur in some cases. Accidents can cause impotence; it can be brought on by depression; and, like a blockage in the bowels or a ruptured appendix, the genital organs can simply malfunction.

Awareness of the potential for impotence varies from man to man. I would say that for the most part it's similar to the way pilots or race-car drivers always listen to the pitch of the engine for the first signs of trouble. After a while it becomes an unconscious act, but if there is the least variation they react.

I can almost guarantee that if you've detected a change in a lover's performance, he knows it too. Proceed with great caution and tact. Give him love. Give him support.

Take the approach that both of you will work to solve the problem as a couple.

We already know that men are not very good at talking about their troubles, and in this case the silence will be deafening. Going to a sex therapist or a psychologist may seem like a perfectly simple thing to do. Yet for men, it is not that easy.

If a woman lets a man know that she understands his sensitivity and approaches it as a "we problem," not a "you problem," there is a better chance that he will seek help. Even then, there will be plenty of resistance. Boys mature into men thinking that they are supposed to "tough it out." The inclination to go it alone is compounded by the feeling that sexual problems don't happen to *real* men.

Men who lose all interest in sex, rather than those who have the desire but not the wherewithal, may be trapped in a deep well of depression. They cannot get out on their own. They need help. And as a friend of mine says, "I took a marriage vow that mentioned something about 'in sickness and in health.' If he is sick, I'm going to be there."

His Dumb Questions Deserve Your Smart Answers

"Was it good for you, honey?" That classic postcoital inquiry has made more trouble than any other six words (trouble that's compounded if the response is, "Why, what happened? I must have dozed off").

It ruins the mood and absolutely throws a bucket of cold water on what was otherwise a lovely, sensual, warm experience. But please understand a couple of things. Number one, he means well. Two, he is reacting to what he thinks women want. He actually thinks he's being sensitive.

For most of human history—all but the last few seconds of it—when men gave a woman's sexual satisfaction more than passing thought, it hinged on winning her admiration and loyalty. Ineffectual lovers stood to lose their women to male rivals. They weren't interested in her pleasure. Contemporary women raised our consciousness by correctly saying, "Hey, what about me?" Well, you were right. We took it to heart, and—remember that we're not very subtle—the annoying question is an attempt at being a more sensitive lover.

And this may come as a surprise, but many times we do not know when you have had an orgasm. Some women, of course, scream and yell and make it sound like Mount Vesuvius erupting, and men aren't so numb that they don't know what that means. It's not nice to eavesdrop, but some friends of mine in Santa Barbara have an apartment with thin walls, and, during parties, their guests are often entertained by a floor show produced by the next-door neighbors. There'd be a loud and prolonged thudding of wood, presumably the headboard of a bed bumping against plaster. It would start slowly and build to a frenzy, and then a woman's voice would shout, "Touchdown!" We all knew that *her* man got the message. But, believe me, there are some women who do not convey the same unmistakable message to a man. I'm not suggesting that you start whooping it up and screeching "Touchdown!" every time you have an orgasm. Just understand that many men are unable to break the code. We don't know for sure, and so we ask a direct question. It's an effort, maybe a clumsy effort, to be considerate. And yes, some men are keeping score or fishing for compliments. Unfortunately, the questions will continue until someone invents a bed with a trapdoor mechanism, activated by a bullshit detector, that drops open whenever a self-styled stud rolls over and asks, "Was it . . ."

Come Now

I've asked men to tell me how important they think it is for a woman to have an orgasm. Here is one quote: "If she has an orgasm, it shows that you did something right." See, he wants to please you. There are some who need to inflate their macho image, yet the vast majority of men, goal- and task-oriented as they are, really want to satisfy you—they are out to do their "duty." Duty doesn't sound very romantic, but men define themselves in just that way.

"Sex is almost a failure if she doesn't have an orgasm" is another quote from my notebook. I saw the quintessential reflection of this attitude during an assignment I had from the *Today* show to report on Nevada's legal brothels. I wanted to learn something important about men and women from those who practice the world's oldest profession, and I asked one of the prostitutes if men expect her to have an orgasm during sexual intercourse. She said that men are constantly trying to arouse her to the point of orgasm. "It's important for them to have me come," she said.

Why? Bragging rights is one factor, obviously. A man looking for a sure sign of virility may think that he's a wonderful stud if he can make a hooker come to climax. But the prostitute told me that she thinks many of her customers think they are supposed to satisfy her. They feel it is what's expected of them.

I couldn't resist asking her whether they ever succeeded. She smiled and said, "Sometimes."

My advice to you is take the question—"Was it good for you?"—the way it was intended. Don't jump all over him. To men, an orgasm is essential; without it, sexual intercourse is incomplete. And while in some Eastern cultures male orgasm is skillfully postponed to prolong and accentuate the ecstasy of lovemaking, it remains the focus of a man's erotic experience. By assuming that orgasm is just as important to a woman, he is trying to pay attention to female sexuality and female needs. They may not have mastered the fine points yet, but it took men several million years to get to this point.

As for an answer, there's the diplomatic "That's one question you don't ever have to ask. You're a wonderful lover." However, if you're not satisfied at that point, ask for more. He'll probably figure that his prowess has tapped a wellspring of passion.

Faking orgasms is an individual thing. As I said earlier, men often can't tell if a woman has had one, and if he doesn't ask, the assumption is that what was supposed to happen did happen. Or, if it didn't happen, he'd just as soon pretend that it did. When a couple has had sex together several times, the partners know each other's bodies and reactions well enough so that guesswork usually isn't necessary. The first time, though, with a large measure of nerves and insecurity on both sides, there can be a lot of question marks.

I listened to a locker-room confession once from a guy who was wondering if his girlfriend was conning him. He told me he had asked her how many orgasms she had experienced (let's hear it for optimists), and her answer was six. A moment went by, she quivered and moaned softly. "Make that seven," she whispered. Was she faking it? Who cares. She's got my nomination for an Oscar.

Before I finish with the subject and close this chapter, I intend to reveal a male secret. Men fake orgasms. After the first explosive ejaculation, it can be difficult to know for sure if a man has reached a climax on a second or third round of lovemaking. There may be sound and fury, but not much else. Without a big orgasmic payoff, men do succumb to the temptation to substitute artifice for effort.

CHAPTER TWELVE

THE "C" WORD— COMMITMENT

Scream the dirty word *commitment* in a crowded men's locker room and there would be a stampede for the door. Or so it seems from all the questions I get about the subject. Usually, they are phrased in the most negative way: "Why are men afraid of making a commitment?"

Many psychologists believe that relationships are not nearly as important to men as they are to women. I agree, and while you probably don't like hearing it put quite so baldly, it's such an important piece of the puzzle that I can't risk being oblique. I told you I'd be your confidant, and that means straight talk.

It's not that relationships are unimportant to men; the point is that they don't rate them the same way women do. Relationships are not our top priority. Probably work would be given a higher position on a scale of one to ten. This is not to say that's where it belongs, but I'm also not suggesting that women are right and men are wrong. I'm noting that there is a difference—there's that word again—in the way men and women order the priorities of life.

I hope enough evidence has piled up to convince you that projecting female standards, ethics, and language onto men leads to great disappointment (yes, men do the same thing to women). We have to keep coming back to that because it is the essence of my message. Women want men to make a commitment, and the way they define the term, what they expect from men, leads them to conclude that we either are afraid of commitment or want to avoid it altogether. Some men are afraid, and some men cut and run; but the sweeping all-purpose conclusion doesn't follow in every case.

Relationships are important to men; not *as* important, but they are important.

One problem is that men and women are operating on different timetables. The trains run on the same tracks but miss the connections. I often find that women are more interested in a permanent commitment earlier in the relationship than a man is. You may have to live with the discrepancy and hold the train in the station until he gets there.

You may be ready to settle down with a guy six months into a relationship, but it may take him eighteen months to make the same decision. That's not open-ended, by the way. At some point you may have to set a deadline and say, "This can't just drift along forever. I love you . . . but *I need* a permanent relationship." Either he responds or he doesn't, but first you do have to give the guy enough time—based on his timetable—before demanding a commitment.

Commitments aren't instant pudding. If the relationship is going to gel it will take longer than five minutes. How long? It varies from couple to couple, but you can help the process along, and ease some of your own frustration, by asking a man where he sees the relationship going in the long run. If you get "Well . . . eh . . . ummm . . . ah . . . hmmm," think seriously about ending it yourself. If he is being vague and slippery, and if it's important for you to have a commitment, there isn't any other acceptable option.

As far as I'm concerned, there is only one kind of stupid question—the question that doesn't get asked. In the early days of a relationship, men and women should be like six-year-olds, asking one question after another. It's the only way to make a stranger into a friend, and a friend into a lover. Ask him about his timetable. Tell him about yours. Ask him about the future, his plans and objectives.

Questions are similar to seeds. An answer may not be instantly ready to harvest, but one may germinate and grow once the question has been asked. Many men tend to be anchored in the present—today is where the action is—and it makes the future a pretty abstract concept. Your questions focus his attention on a subject that's always been on tomorrow's agenda. By asking, you transform the future into the present.

The answer will give you a rough idea of when the train will arrive, and whether it's an express or a local that makes all the stops. And ask yourself a few questions: Is it worth the wait? Can I afford to wait? Am I on the right track?

Playing the Waiting Game

In order to get from Point A to Point B, it helps to understand the quirks of the transportation system. What women regard as a man's fear of commitment is often an uncoordinated trolley-car line called love. I rode on it myself and jumped off at the "marriage station," only to find that the woman I loved was not there yet. She was headed in the right direction and eventually arrived, but it was frustrating, and the experience gave me a certain amount of empathy with women who end up waiting on an empty platform. It also made me skeptical about the men-won't-make-commitments putdown. The rate of marriages has gone up in the last decade, and unless I've got it wrong, for every bride there is a groom. During the height of the cold war, everything was blamed on the Russians. Too much rain—the Russians. Too cold—the Russians. Now we have another useful all-purpose explanation when things don't come out the way we want them to: "Men just won't make commitments."

The Magic Number

I do not know what it is about the number six, but many women have told me that they start to look for their relationships to solidify after about six months. Dana expects to have spent at least two weekends at the home of a guy's parents by the end of a six-month period (she says to beware of men who keep you away from their family). Kelly arranges to have a conversation about children before the six-month anniversary rolls around (she says it separates the men from the boys). And Jane, after one ultimately unsuccessful live-in relationship, told the next man in her life that she wouldn't allow their affair to drag on past six months without the prospect of a permanent commitment.

The score is two for three. Dana got engaged after a Christmas at Ed's family home in Montana. Jane is married. And Kelly's baby talk continues to separate out the boys without turning up a man (she still believes in the six-month rule, though).

Synchronizing Your Watches

My buddy Ken has a lot going for him, but subtlety is not one of his strong points and it helped wreck his relationship with Elizabeth.

He was in love, thoroughly and completely. Sadly, he was unable to communicate that fact to the woman who needed to know it. They dated for months, she kept her own place, but there were many nights at Ken's house, and the two of them spent the bulk of their free time together. Elizabeth moved some of her clothes into Ken's closets, and he gave her one of the bathrooms as a private preserve. All of this, as far as Ken was concerned, was a commitment. Through his actions, he was saying, "You're it. You're my kind of woman."

The problem was that he should have come right out and said it instead of playing the strong, silent type. Ken did not realize that Elizabeth needed to hear the words, hear him express his love and commitment to her. Ken's "sign language" wasn't enough. But Elizabeth also failed to communicate. She never told Ken that she was beginning to wonder why he was so reluctant to be up front about their relationship. She wanted to know about their future, but Ken was living in the present, taking it one day at a time. The uncertainty slowly poisoned the relationship. It was marriage that Elizabeth wanted. Nothing short of an unprompted proposal would have saved Ken in her eyes.

Elizabeth knew things were going downhill. She hoped that Ken would realize it too and do something. But Ken continued to speak in sign language. As far as he was concerned, Elizabeth was happy. Didn't they still spend their free time together at his house? Hadn't she set up her word processor in the back bedroom? Wasn't the sex great?

When Elizabeth finally told Ken she was leaving, he went into a deep depression. I had never seen him so down, and I went over to Elizabeth's apartment in the hopes that I could get the couple back together. We talked for several hours. Much of what I heard wasn't news. It had been obvious for months that Ken wasn't paying enough attention to Elizabeth's needs.

The next day, during an unusually vicious racquet-ball game, I gave Ken a hard workout while relating Elizabeth's side of the story. While I showered, he called her and offered to put her name on the deed to his house. He told her to redecorate the place any way she wanted (the one stipulation was that the TV and piano had to stay). The back bedroom could be her exclusive domain for writing projects. Eventually, they'd buy another house.

More sign language. Ken was trying, but he was still not speaking Elizabeth's language. Their definitions of commitment were completely different. He thought commitment was sharing a house, sharing fun, and sharing a bed. And Ken was sexually exclusive with Elizabeth, which, to him, was equivalent to giving up his right arm. He was so smitten by her that he was willing to drop his friendships with other women. And he really meant it. Ken told me that he had no interest in being with another woman, and, knowing him as well as I did, that came as a tremendous shock. This is a man who believes that, when it comes to sex, "you either use it or lose it." He is handsome, charming, and a celebrity in his hometown.

Before Elizabeth made her decision to break off the

relationship, I fully expected to attend the couple's wedding one day. I understood Ken's language, but she did not. I arranged a dinner for them, hoping that things could still be salvaged, and Ken opened up—promising to take action on the points that he considered crucial to the relationship. But his ideas and her ideas about the relationship and commitment were still out of synch. Elizabeth told Ken that his actions—and his words—had come too late.

In retrospect, I think Elizabeth's confidence in Ken started to drain away early in the relationship, when she expected him to propose marriage. If Elizabeth had waited for an opportune moment and told Ken what *she* wanted out of the relationship, the outcome might have been different. Although Ken was on the mend from a painful divorce and the subject of marriage would probably not have been a real thrill, at least he would have been alerted to Elizabeth's feelings. In turn, he could have explained his reluctance to plunge into another marriage so soon after the divorce. Elizabeth might have seen that Ken's lack of commitment—what she interpreted as a lack of commitment—was not motivated by second thoughts about her.

Ultimately, this could-would-should game I am playing with the case of Ken and Elizabeth proves my central point. Even in the end, when it was too late, Elizabeth could not bring herself to tell Ken what it was that she wanted out of the relationship. She kept him guessing and left him guessing.

Who was to blame? There's plenty of it to go around, but that's not my job. What is my job is to help, as best I can, to get the trains to run on time. Ken and Elizabeth did not make the necessary connection. Her train left the station before his arrived. She was on eastern daylight, while he chugged along on mountain standard.

Biding His Time, Biding Your Time

Many times, commitment is a function of age. To get a commitment from a young man, one who is in his twenties, he must overcome his fear that he is being asked to choose between his career and a relationship. During that particular time of life it is tough to get guys to focus on things that are not related to the job. They're busy learning the ropes and gathering professional credentials. Energy levels are high, and it's no big deal to put in a twelve- or fifteen-hour day.

Between the ages of twenty-six and about thirty, when the career is starting to get into shape, men start warming up to the idea of commitment. At that point they are more interested in sharing their lives with a woman; there is something to share, for one thing.

Another angle on the age factor is simple biology. Men tend to remain sexually active and fertile into their sixth and seventh decades. Men don't feel the same time pressure to begin raising a family before it's too late. Don't get me wrong. Men want love with all of its security and nourishment, just as women do, but they also want control; for them, it's part of being an adult.

Heading for Home

By going through the motions, pretending to love, or faking a commitment, some men believe that they can have both control and a satisfactory relationship with a woman.

Sharing, however, is such a central element in any healthy relationship that if he can't share responsibility—won't share control with the person he is supposed to love—the blank spot cannot be hidden by smooth talk and romantic gestures.

Manipulative, abusive behavior is a symptom of a neurotic obsession for control. Most of us, though, learn that there is a valuable payoff for letting go. The best analogy is one I heard from a man who had plunged into love; falling in love is too mild a term. He said the experience was "like going home again." And what a great image that is! We can all go home again if we are willing to make a commitment and to love.

Even so, there is a real ambivalence at work, and you can understand what's going on by keeping in mind that men and women tend to fear the things they want most. The greater the fear, the greater the desire. We erect an iron curtain around our deepest desires because we are afraid to face the consequences of obtaining them.

Therefore, to obtain your love, which he desires, a man fears that the consequence will be a loss of control, something he has been struggling to gain since childhood. And if he is a young man, in his early to mid-twenties, he is still bleeding from the wounds suffered during his painful wars of adolescent rebellion, and the idea of commitment can be terrifying.

Trivial Pursuits

Here's a scene that I think you can appreciate; it's one that my father, Bernard Berkowitz, the psychoanalyst and co-author of *How to Be Your Own Best Friend*, says is typical of men who are struggling to retain control: There's a couple sitting in the living room. The guy is watching TV and decides the room is getting a little too warm. He gets up to turn on the air-conditioner. He's in the act of reaching for the switch and his wife, without looking up from her reading, says, "While you're up, why don't you turn on the air-conditioner?" He stops dead in his tracks. Turning on the air-conditioner now involves doing his wife's bidding. He may argue that the room is perfectly comfortable, that the electric bills are too high, or he may open the window—all tactics to reestablish control over something that was trivial in the first place. When I tell this story to men, they always nod and indicate that they've done exactly the same kind of thing.

And I've noticed a few women nodding too. Men *and* women have mixed feelings about giving up control. Even so, I've heard a lot about how men don't want to grow up. This explains—so the theory goes—why men can't make commitments. The *Peter Pan Syndrome* was used as the title for a popular self-help book. Peter was the boy who rescued Wendy and the other children from Captain Hook; he could fly, but he couldn't and wouldn't grow up.

This is a stereotype about men that's taken hold in recent years. Whenever I try it out on men, individually or in groups, the notion gets shot down. Men are in a hurry to grow up and to take charge of their lives. Why? Because childhood is a prolonged state of dependence, not a fantasy land where boys can fly and fight pirates.

Becoming independent is such an overriding goal that we have trouble coming to terms with the control-versus-commitment paradox. How do women manage to do it? Good question; one that I've asked dozens of experts, and I've gotten dozens of different answers, ranging from "Biology is destiny" to "Social conditioning" to "Luck" and, finally, to "Beats me."

A few years ago, Sal, the owner of a favorite Washington, D.C., restaurant where I was dining with friends, came over to our table to chat. He mentioned that he was about to be married, and someone teased him about "getting caught." Sal shook his head, "The other way around," he said. "I had to catch her. I was the one who wanted to get married . . . she wasn't interested." Sal said he needed to know that they were married.

Nobody had to tell Sal that making commitments is a risky, difficult business, and that it isn't made any easier by the changes in social patterns that have taken place in recent decades. We've lost some of those cultural crossroads that mark the natural stages in life where commitment and marriage seem almost inevitable. Getting married right out of high school was once routine. Senior year in college used to be associated with sheepskins and engagement rings. And coming back from military service was another one of those moments that suggested it was time to "settle down." Now we take it one day at a time until we realize that the varsity basketball jacket has mysteriously grown smaller and won't zip up anymore.

Making Haste Slowly with Divorced Men

Be cautious with men who are ready for a commitment right after a divorce or the breakup of a long relationship. I once worked with a guy who was a great example of a man on the rebound. And in his case, he was prematurely rebounding, since he was having an affair with another woman while his marriage was disintegrating. Eventually there was a divorce, and he immediately proposed to his girlfriend. They were married in a flash. Around the office we called her Cindy II because she was a dead ringer for Cindy I, the ex-wife. They could have been physical and emotional twins.

I warned Marty to think twice and even consider professional counseling to figure out what went wrong with the first marriage before plunging into the second. Obviously, he had subconscious needs that he wanted fulfilled in the second marriage and which hadn't been resolved the first time around. Incidentally, Cindy II has given way to Cindy III, or, for all I know, Cindy IV.

I'm not saying that all divorced men are poison, but give them time, and a minimum of a year is not unreasonable, to get their heads back together. Think of it as painting the outside of a house. You don't do it right after the place has been drenched in a thunderstorm. Wait for the sun to come out and dry the shingles.

Walk This Way

Meg is a fashion model, and is she ever stunning. Heads turn—male and female—when she enters a room. And her personality matches her looks. She's intelligent, has a great sense of humor, and is as even-tempered and sweet as they come. Yet Meg is engaged to a guy who is abusive. He doesn't beat her, not physically, but his verbal punches are aimed at her self-esteem.

What happens is this: Without warning, Meg's apartment will be "raided" by her boyfriend. He'll drop by to make sure she is not with another man. It happens any time of the night or day. He calls constantly, and if she's not quick to answer or—God forbid—isn't there, he flies into a jealous rage. He yells and screams, rants and raves.

"Why," I asked Meg, "do you take this kind of stuff?"

"I don't know. I guess I love him," she said with a shrug of her shoulders.

Here is a woman who could have any man in the world—she's got brains and poise and beauty and everything else. Even so, Meg will put up with an incredible amount of nonsense because she thinks that if she tells this loser to go play in the polar bear cage at the zoo there will never be another man in her life. It's as if there is a voice out there warning, "This is it, Meg. Last call. They don't get any better than him."

Come off it! If he has the personality of a concentration-camp guard, say good-bye and good riddance. Don't look back. Staying in an abusive relationship one minute longer than necessary is potentially crippling. It destroys confidence, the one characteristic that is at the core of any healthy relationship. If you don't have confidence in yourself and respect yourself, men who wouldn't dream of abusing a woman are likely to keep their distance. "He's my last chance" can turn out to be a self-fulfilling prophesy.

But notice that I said staying in an abusive relationship *one minute longer than necessary* is potentially crippling. Sometimes there is no quick and easy way out. There may be children to protect, or economic factors to be weighed. Jumping from the frying pan of an abusive relationship (and I'm still talking about nonphysical abuse) into the fire of homelessness or destitution is not a good idea. It could take time and careful planning to extricate yourself from a bad situation.

Meg, however, and Brenda, who works as a paralegal in a Miami law office, do not face such stark alternatives.

Brenda and I had a talk about men and commitment. She wanted to know how she could get Donald, her live-in boyfriend, to make a commitment. Now, get this: Donald has moved in to her place, but Brenda pays all the rent and buys the groceries, cooks, and cleans. He doesn't do anything but sit in front of the TV night after night.

I thought about it a little while and then something clicked. Why in the world did she want that kind of a guy to make a commitment? The only kind of commitment I'd want from him is "Promise me you'll leave and never come back."

There is no special male quality to Don's behavior. He is a parasite, and the species comes in male and female varieties. This male parasite was living off Brenda. In another situation, he could be mooching from Randy. We can get bogged down in esoteric questions about a man's financial responsibility to the woman in his life, but why bother? Brenda was not asking for a rent check. She wanted an adult relationship.

I asked Brenda if she would put up with that kind of exploitation from another woman or even a relative, and, of course, she said no. Bad manners are bad manners; rudeness is rudeness. It doesn't matter if it's Don or Deb or Dad.

Wouldn't life alone be better than life with somebody like Don? And if the answer is anything other than YES! your problem is not one of getting a commitment from a man. The problem is rebuilding your sense of self-worth. If you don't love yourself and make a commitment to yourself, men won't love you or make a commitment to you either.

There is a lot of pain involved in breaking off dead-end relationships. All of us prefer to avoid pain, but we're only making excuses when the facts of an abusive relationship are staring us in the face and we refuse to see them. Women have the power to control their own lives, but they've got to be willing to use it. In Brenda's case, turning off Don's TV and tearing up his meal ticket would be the place to start.

Every behavior pattern has a source or starting point. A man who has been fired from a job might turn abusive, but that does not justify what he is doing to a lover or spouse. Alcoholism, drug abuse, and mental illness are different matters, though. If he is undergoing treatment and making an effort to recover, he needs your help. If possible, stay with him—but only, only if he is undergoing treatment. It is the illness that is undercutting the relationship, and as long as it is being treated, then there is hope.

Going a Long Way on a Little Research

Short of visiting a tarot card reader, it's tough to gauge whether the man you're interested in is the "committing kind." One thing you can do is to listen to what he says about an ex-wife or ex-girlfriend. If he is over sixteen, you're probably not the first woman in his life. Ask him a few questions about what went wrong (maybe nothing went wrong, and you will have to solve the mystery of why he's not happily married with three kids). Don't interrogate him KGB-style, but gently ask the right questions: "How come things didn't work out?" "When did the problems start?" And really open your ears so that you can hear the warning bells ringing in the distance. Once you've discussed his past, talk about his future. What does he want to do with his life? Where does he go from here? In the early days of a relationship, you shouldn't expect to see your name written into the script in capital letters. It's probably too early for that. But you'll be able to tell whether he is planning a long-running one-man show. To make the point, here's an example I picked up on a flight to Salt Lake City. The guy sitting next to me was a doctor. To while away the time, one of our bits of small talk involved the difficulty of balancing the demands of a job with the demands of a family. Bill Cooper said he loved his work and made it a rule to tell all of his girlfriends that he would never let anything get in the way of his career as a surgeon. He has been married three times, and his ex-wives all blame the breakups on Dr. Cooper's workaholic tendencies. "They can't say I didn't warn them," he said as the plane banked steeply on its final approach.

Another method is more indirect. It's based on the them-versus-us formula. Compare notes with him about other couples. Why are Ned and Carrie having so many problems? Why do Alice and Gary seem so happy? His answers and analyses may be more self-revealing than he realizes.

Films and books can offer insights. What does he enjoy reading and seeing on the screen? Are his favorite cinema heroes always "real men," loners, love-'em-and-leave-'em types? Literature and drama deal with many of the cutting-edge issues that are important to a relationship. Talk to him about the denouement, the plot twists, the conflict facing the characters and how it's resolved. A guy who hates Annie Hall may not be your kind of guy (or maybe he is). Life, it has been said, imitates art.

Above all else, listen closely. Sometimes we're so overcome with love that emotions plug up our ears and smother our logic. Listen dispassionately and you will learn a lot about how he feels about the "C" word.

CHAPTER THIRTEEN

THE DOWNSIDE

Question: Why don't men have the same kind of close, intimate, caring relationships with their men friends that women have with their women friends?

Answer: As I said earlier in the book, men are not very good at verbalizing. When men get together, often they don't say very much, but they kind of know how they feel. Slaps on the back, the high fives in sports, patting a hitter on the butt as he heads for the dugout, are nonverbal means of communication that men use all the time.

Aside from this preference for an elbow in the ribs rather than a heart-to-heart chat, men suffer from homophobia. Men have a much greater fear of being accused of being homosexual than women do. Two women who haven't seen each other for months can meet on the street and exchange hugs and kisses without the slightest awkwardness. Nobody thinks twice about it. You can still go into a disco and see women dancing together. Women walking arm-in-arm are not unusual in any American city. They have "permission" to wear men's clothes—hats, suits, shoes, sweaters. But men do not have that same permission in our society.

In a men's locker room, nobody, but nobody, looks below the Adam's apple when it's shower time. It's just bad form. Men worry about giving the impression that they're gay. It's unfortunate, but in large part it explains the fear of developing close male friendships. Crying on another guy's shoulder is just too dangerous, and when it happens there is usually a ritual involved, such as sports, that removes the potential taint of homosexuality. Real men can cry when they lose the World Series. They hug and slap each other after taking the big game.

Women are not afraid to look at each other's bodies, to touch, to hug, to dance, to sleep in the same bed. The result is that women are more comfortable together.

The men, however, will avoid making contact with each other, and if there is contact they will worry for days afterward that they've gone over the line and become gay. The instinct is to push away from it to such an extent that close male friendships are difficult.

It's another form of homophobia. I know a couple of guys who ended up in a hotel room that had only one double bed. There was no other choice and so they shared the bed; at least they didn't flip a coin to see who was going to sleep on the floor or in the bathtub. But they were very uneasy; afterward, they avoided each other for several weeks to prove that they weren't "strange."

Question: Why do men resent a female boss?

Answer: Fear. Most of us—men and women—fear the unknown. When we don't know what to expect, we start to dream up worst-case scenarios. For men in their mid-forties, fifties, and older, the idea of having to contend with women as career competitors awakens all sorts of uncertainty, insecurity, and fear. They don't know what to expect from women on the job and so they react with hostility.

A guy who has put ten or fifteen years into a company is very vulnerable these days. Leveraged buyouts and mergers mean that there will be fewer jobs to go around. Cost-cutting measures bear down on those with the highest salaries. Just because you're paranoid doesn't mean that you don't have any enemies. And the enemy ends up being the women who are just starting their climb up the corporate ladder.

It's easy to develop a siege mentality—us versus them. If you're one of "them," nothing is going to be good enough. Record sales figures, satisfied clients, new accounts, won't matter.

But time is on your side. Retirements and layoffs are making openings for women. And men are learning, slowly, that they can co-exist with women in the workplace. Younger men seem to be able to adapt a little better, probably because they are not old enough to have worked in places where women were either excluded or relegated to the secretarial pool.

In the end, once the fear subsides, and once the necessary adjustments are made, men will begin to judge women by the standards they apply to themselves—performance and the achievement of goals.

Role Models and Rolling the Models

Caroline, a lobbyist for a major trade association in Washington, D.C., tells me that the top executive positions in her organization are all filled by men. She is philosophical about the situation, however. The second tier of management is gradually being filled by women. Traditionally, those jobs have been the stepping-stones to the senior spots, and when a fast-track male tries to jump over the second tier and grab a juicy assignment, his effectiveness is diminished because he lacks the hands-on job experience. Ironically, the power plays have made the women look good in comparison.

What's helping the trade-association women in their upward climb, according to Caroline, is the growing presence of women in powerful government jobs. Congress, the White House, and even the Supreme Court are no longer exclusive men's clubs. "My male colleagues," she told me, "are beginning to realize that I can get my phone calls returned too." And I wouldn't be surprised if Caroline has a White House post one of these days.

Winning professional respect is essential. Men don't automatically get it the moment they walk in the front door of the office. If you want to tame the lions, you'd better show them you can handle a whip and a chair. Sadly, women are going to have to work even harder than their male counterparts. The lions aren't used to having a woman in the same cage. And, by the way, neither are other women. I've seen women in top jobs take some of their heaviest flak from other women, and as a result they end up fighting for their careers on two fronts.

It's important to choose your issues and battles carefully on a case-by-case basis. A sexist joke in one context can be a call-to-arms, and absolutely nothing to laugh at. In another moment or setting that same joke can be worth a chuckle. Mature judgment is what it's all about.

Overt sexist actions are another thing. Those can't be tolerated. There's no room for discrimination on the job.

But remember that we're a country that thrives on humor: ethnic, racial, sexual. Just about anything is inbounds. It's a social mechanism; we reach for a joke instead of a gun. If you're climbing the corporate ladder, I can assure you that you will be teased and tweaked and twitted all the way to the top. Take it, have some fun, and give it right back to them.

Question: Why do men visit brothels?

Answer: The simple, glib, and truthful answer is that they go to a whorehouse because they are not getting what they want at home. Now, I'm not saying that it's a legitimate alternative to marital sex. The question was, Why do men visit brothels? I'm not going to tell you it's because they like the wallpaper, or that there's some deep desire to despoil women.

Flip back to Chapter Two where I said that men are simpler than women think. He may go to a bordello to get oral sex, which is something that he likes. It could be that there's nothing more to it than that.

I'm not advising you to slavishly follow his sexual agenda. If you're not comfortable with what he wants, then don't do it or seek counseling. But the point is that men go to prostitutes because they have a specific need and the prostitutes fill that need in exchange for money.

I think that in some cases where his self-esteem is dicey, if he has an ego problem, he may go to a brothel to demonstrate that "by God, this is a place where I'm in charge and I get what I want."

Remember what I said about relationships and how they are not as high a priority for many men? With a prostitute men can pay their money and get sexual gratification without having to worry about commitment, emotional involvement, or another person's feelings. Value in exchange for money; no-fault sex.

In the course of the reporting assignment that took me to Nevada's legal brothels, I learned that men often went to the "ranches," as they're called, to talk. Sure, they were there for the sex, but the communications part was very important. The prostitutes told me that they become good friends and advisers to many of their customers.

These places have nice cocktail lounges; you could be in any trendy fern bar. I met an old gent who was easily in his seventies. He said that he came regularly to have sex because his wife was too ill and infirm to make love. And it was his wife's idea for him to go to the bordello.

There is a long list of good reasons why this is a compassionate but questionable idea. There are health risks, although the owners of Nevada's legal brothels insist that their standards of hygiene are strict and rigorously enforced. But over the years, the danger of venereal disease has kept many and maybe even the majority of men away from illicit establishments elsewhere. Now, with AIDS, the danger is a million times more acute.

The use of condoms is required at the legal brothels, and when I talked to one of the women about the subject, I picked up a fascinating anecdote. She told me that the condom not only protected her health but her marriage as well. Knowing that there was that thin rubber membrane between his wife and a customer allowed her husband the peace of mind to live with her occupation. He didn't like it, but they needed the money she was earning, and the condom made it okay.

And his illusion brings us full circle to the question: Why do men visit brothels? Sex is magical; it plays tricks on us. Few things have such power to distort reality. Like the prostitute's husband, who was convinced that the condom redeems the sale of his wife's body, the men who go to the ranches persuade themselves that they can find love and friendship and an antidote to the loneliness that grips their lives.

CHAPTER FOURTEEN

HIS CHEATING HEART

Men are born window-shoppers. We like to check out the merchandise as it walks by on the street. That doesn't mean we intend to buy. Looking at other women is not an act of infidelity.

I asked my wife whether she objected to my wandering eyes. "Does it bother you," I wanted to know, "if I look at a beautiful woman who's passing by?"

She said, "No, I'd think you were blind if you didn't," but quickly added, "as long as looking is all that you're doing." I nodded thoughtfully to signal that I took note of the distinction before changing the subject.

Let's not be hypocrites. Women look at other women; why shouldn't men do the same? And women look at other men as well. I've been in the *Today* show's greenroom, the area where the guests wait to go on the air. If a woman comes through the front door, before she has advanced six feet, every other woman in the room will have critically examined the outfit she's wearing, her shoes, her makeup, and her hair, not to mention having made a few appreciative comments about the good-looking guy she is with. Sweeping conclusions will be drawn about her status, educational level, IQ, and morals. The men, in the meantime, if they've even looked up from their newspapers, have noted a totally different set of characteristics, and most of what they've perceived is tied to her sexuality. To put it bluntly, in those first few seconds she is a sex object.

Men who make a big deal of ogling every woman in sight and mouthing off for the world to hear are rude. They embarrass other men, as a matter of fact. I get annoyed when I pass construction sites and hear all the noises that are directed at women on the street, and I certainly wouldn't want to be bombarded with "Baby, baby, baby . . . please, baby, please," gross noises, and outright obscenities. But I have noticed that when the banter is playful and light, those guys occasionally get waves and winks and teasing comments in response.

There is no law against asking a man what it is he likes about the woman he is admiring. I don't mean stopping a hard hat to inquire if it's your long legs that he's screaming about. My wife will say to me, "I didn't know you liked short hair." And she is making note of what it is that's grabbing my attention. A week later I could easily come home to find that Mr. Lorenzo has whacked a couple of inches off the top or that the clothes closet is newly stocked with several of the short skirts that have been straining my eyesight.

Learning that a man goes for "substantial" women by watching what he's watching on the street could save you a lot of money on diet books. Ask him if he would like you to try that look. If he says yes, get out the phone book and start making reservations at four-star restaurants.

Making Use of a Man's Best Instincts

Wandering eyes are easy to spot, but a wandering body is not nearly so obvious. How do you know when a man is cheating?

A sudden change in well-established behavior patterns and habits is one sign. An inexplicable exercise binge or clothes-shopping spree may mean that he is getting restless.

But I don't believe that women have to become detectives staking out their husbands, waiting for clues to drop. Infidelity is symptomatic of other problems. Look for those problems and attempt to solve them before the infidelity sets in.

Shere Hite claims that 70 percent of the women who have been married for more than five years engage in extramarital affairs. And she lets them off the hook by saying that those women are seeking something that is lacking in their married lives. Many men are in the exact same position. They are after emotional or sexual satisfaction and attention that is absent at home.

One missing ingredient may be the sense that he is needed to provide protection, strength, and sustenance to the family or relationship. Every man wants to know that he is a "take charge" kind of guy. It's a key part of our self-image and historic role. This is sort of a reassuring subconscious shadow that we all have, and when it is lost, men may go looking to find it.

Often, younger, less-accomplished women provide men with the illusion that they are the protector, the mentor, the guide. And it may not be an illusion, either. A mature man has a lot of experience and wisdom to offer someone who has just enrolled in the school of hard knocks.

What is an illusion, though, is the sense of renewal and permanence that is generated by splicing generations together over such a wide span of years. The student doesn't stay in school forever.

Keep your curiosity alive about him and his work. Men don't usually confide in other men, but they do have an urge to let down their guard and examine the important aspects of life with the woman they love. Some of it may not be your idea of fun, but if you look bored or preoccupied, he probably won't share much of himself. The couples who sit together in silence at restaurant tables seem to have run out of things to talk about, while the young lovers around them—and being a young lover is not a function of age—nearly drown out the dinner music with their conversation and laughter. They've got a million questions to ask each other and billions of ideas to try out. People who expect each day to yield the same old thing get exactly that—the same old thing.

Cheating Figures

Whenever I see a graph or a chart, I remind myself that there are "lies, damned lies and statistics." But unfortunately, the statistics on marital infidelity have the ring of truth to them. There's a whole lot of cheating going on.

Usually, infidelity is presented as a male phenomenon, but the growth end of the cheating industry is women. Recent studies confirm the trend, although getting accurate data isn't easy and it will be years, if ever, before women overtake men and lose their status as the sex that is most sinned against by sinful partners.

The old answers explaining why men cheat have outworn their usefulness. You've heard them all: Men cheat because they are lechers; men cheat because they hate women; men cheat because they're trying to prove that they are still young; etc. At bottom, I get the feeling that in this area it has always been necessary to brand men as somehow uniquely deranged and dirty.

But if the statistics are right and women are following men down the crooked path to extramarital affairs, there must be another explanation. One theory that's been advanced by feminist groups is that women are reacting to a lack of intimate and fulfilling relationships and seeking them elsewhere. It's plausible; so plausible, in fact, that a similar line of reasoning could also be advanced to explain why men are unfaithful.

However, "She made me do it" is as lame as "He made me do it."

Let's strip away the moral absolutes and think in terms of a straightforward cause and effect to explain infidelity. Traditionally, men have cheated because they've had more opportunities to cheat. They've spent most of their lives outside the home. Now women are living and working under the same conditions. They have more opportunities to cheat than before—do I hear an echo?—and, therefore, the infidelity statistics are going up.

Women are out where the action is, earning a paycheck. Philandering, these days, is an equal-opportunity enterprise. We are all capable of cheating, and cheating is being done by both sexes.

As commonsensical as this observation may be, it's probably not very comforting. Still, you may feel better knowing that we are talking about human frailty rather than an incurable and exclusively male "disease."

Those who fall off the fidelity wagon usually climb back

on and stay there. They are not compulsive cheaters. In many cases, the transgression happened without planning, malice aforethought, or whatever. It was just one of those crazy things. Remember the Yiddish proverb I cited earlier: "His brains got soft."

Registering a Pattern

Control and confirmation are two reasons that psychologists often cite for infidelity. Both men and women need ego reinforcement, and as a relationship evolves, the quantity and quality of this nourishment can change.

As a relationship matures it gets more complex, and complications have a way of generating frustrations (I'll bet you've noticed). As the frustrations mount, there is a deepening sense that control is being lost. What can attract a man into an extramarital affair is the fantasy notion that the complications can be wiped out and control regained.

Sexual intercourse with a new partner is exciting. The blast of passion provides confirmation that a man is a man, not just in a sexual sense but in terms of being loved, admired, and worthy of another person's desire. The beginning of a new affair has the hint of déjà vu about it; there is a reminder of other times, other loves, that once seemed so perfect and glorious.

In the last few sentences, I've focused on men and infidelity. But I could have been writing about women as well. The infidelity patterns are similar. I'm reminded of an old line that applies equally to both sexes: Everything I enjoy doing is either illegal, immoral, or fattening.

Collage Education

Every now and then I come down with the jitters. Journalists often get into trouble for delivering unwelcome news, but it is an occupational hazard. I've formed a sort of collage of comments from men who cheat on their wives or steady girlfriends in order to give my readers a look at the rationalization process that is involved. I'm not—repeat, *not*—holding up any of it as a handy way to explain away infidelity. I've changed initials and given the men occupations that approximate their career status.

W.D., a travel agent: "I can turn back the clock. Every time I make love with a new woman, I'm seventeen years old again."

T.N., an editorial cartoonist: "I'm the guy who can't say no. If I were a woman, I'd have ten kids."

R.P., a florist: "It's an adventure . . . a little dangerous. There's not much of that left in life anymore."

S.O., a basketball coach: "Sex is another game, I guess."

N.S., a veterinarian: "I got bored and depressed and needed a lift."

What I didn't put into the collage was the so-called sex addict. I'm not convinced that such a condition exists. Addictions have physiological roots. Dependence on drugs and alcohol are examples. Having talked with sex therapists and marriage counselors, my impression is that the sex "addict" is wrestling with an emotional problem.

I have known men, though, who behave like they are gripped by an addiction when it comes to sex. John, a State Department foreign service officer, would frequently interrupt important diplomatic assignments for the sake of an assignation. He'd miss airline connections, skip embassy meetings, and disappear for hours at a time while he was pursuing a new lover. John knew he was damaging his career but seemed not to care.

He was also an alcoholic, and a severe illness forced him to face up to his alcoholism. In the course of his alcohol-abuse treatment he got control of the self-destructive sexual behavior patterns. John's case suggests that both "addictions" were, at least in part, generated by psychological sources. After a time, the craving for alcohol dug in and took the form of a clearly defined addiction; his body needed the alcohol to function, and the alcoholism gave John an excuse for philandering as well as a cover for the stigma of being a drunk. He could pretend that he was a playboy when convenient, or fall back on the "I was blasted and couldn't help myself" line when he got caught with his pants down.

While "I cheated on you because I'm a sex addict" isn't any more convincing, habitual promiscuity probably needs professional attention.

The Price of Cheating

Most married men don't go around looking to cheat. Rational people avoid trouble, and an extramarital affair is a whole lot of trouble. There is the emotional stress, the guilt that comes from inflicting a wound on another person, the potential loss of a loving family, and the real possibility of financial ruin in a divorce court.

A few moments of sexual pleasure are not worth the potential price, and, yet, cheating still occurs. Reread the preceding paragraph, and you will see that I used the word *rational* in the second sentence; it's the key to understanding the infidelity riddle. Sex is the ultimate irrational act.

Cheating is another layer of irrationality, like the muck that builds up along a river bank after each flood. What should you do if it happens? Look out for the quicksand. Be rational.

Ask yourself this question: If someone makes one mistake, is it worth blowing a good marriage? All of us are capable of falling off the fidelity wagon. There are a lot of temptations in this world. Based on my conversations with men who have cheated, and with women who have struggled to cope with that breach of faith, I would say that the most successful course of action is to express your anger and disappointment, but don't immediately push the plunger and destroy the marriage.

The couples that survived tended to be the ones that confronted the problem head on. She told him what the risks would be if the cheating happened again. He took a good, hard look at the price tag. Men are accustomed to living and working in a cause-and-effect world. "If you do X, I will do Y" is something we understand very well.

And if it does happen again, you must follow through; otherwise, the vicious circle of irrationality takes over.

Two Wrongs = Two Wrongs

While the thought of cheating a cheater seems appealing, it's a bad idea. There are several good reasons for having sexual intercourse. Among other things, it's fun. But revenge or punishment are not good reasons. There's just too much at stake.

Most men feel guilty when they stray. They have failed and the failure hurts. A few years ago, I was drinking beer with a colleague at a seedy bar in the red-light district of Buenos Aires. The place was crawling with hookers and he couldn't resist. But a half hour later, after he paid his money and took his chances upstairs, my friend was back at the bar and almost in tears. He felt horrible about betraying his wife. And for what? A few minutes of being masturbated by a stranger. As far as I know, he's never made the same mistake again.

If his wife had learned about the episode and retaliated in kind, what would have been accomplished? The original infidelity can't be erased. He was a one-time loser, but even a habitual cheater would sail blithely on, from bed to bed, none the wiser. Sex is too important to waste on revenge.

Honesty May Not Always Be the Best Policy

What happens if the fidelity wagon hits a pothole and you fall off? My advice is, if the affair was a once-in-a-lifetime thing, it is not a good idea to turn state's evidence against yourself. A husband or a lover does not really need to know that you strayed. If you insist on making a confession to him, ask yourself whether it's for his benefit or for the sake of relieving your own guilt feelings (or wounding him).

I've seen survey data that shows that roughly half the men polled would be willing to forgive their wives if they caught them cheating. Those figures came as a surprise to me, and I wonder if the respondents were trying to win points with the researchers by providing an answer that they thought would show them to be "liberated" men.

It is difficult to find men who will admit that they have been cheated on, and when I do, they are usually bubbling caldrons of emotion. The husbands of rape victims often can't bring themselves to have sex with their wives. And those women are mutilated casualties of a violent crime, not adulterers.

Private detectives are kept in business by jealous husbands. One rent-a-sleuth told me that women rarely ask for surveillance on a husband who is suspected of infidelity. Most of the time it's a man who wants to know the terrible truth, and when he arrives in the detective's office he tosses a pair of his wife's panties on the desk. While it sounds like a move right out of an X-rated Raymond Chandler flick, word has gotten around that labs can find traces of semen on the fabric.

My recommendation is to think about those panties on the desk top when you're tempted to make a confession. Coming clean is good for the soul, but it is not good for a relationship and not good for a man's ego. The urge to talk out a dilemma can be satisfied by putting your thoughts down on paper. You are organizing your ideas and venting emotions when you write. It's useful to wait a few days and then go back when things are calmer and reread pages that may have been written when a traumatic moment was reaching the flood stage. You may see options, opportunities, glimmers of hope, that were overlooked the first time around.

By all means guard your diary, but if he catches you straying, don't expect him to be any calmer or more reasonable than you would be under the same circumstances (at a minimum). The objective is to get things on a rational basis as quickly as possible so that you both can examine why the incident happened in the first place. Professional counseling is helpful in this regard.

If the affair was the equivalent of a fender bender, an accident that's not likely to happen again, don't tell him if he hasn't noticed the scratches, and don't make any more left turns out of the right lane.

Crime Between the Sheets

If there is a bottom line, it's this: The standards of sexual behavior change with each generation. Every night things happen in respectable bedrooms all over America that would have been grounds for divorce fifty years ago, let alone exposing the perpetrators to criminal charges. The hard-and-fast rules of what's right and what's wrong aren't quite so hard or nearly so fast. Each of us may want to build in some flexibility to allow our own ideas and lives to bend without breaking in the winds of change, the way that tall buildings ride out sudden winter storms.

CHAPTER FIFTEEN

WORD PLAY

The dictionary is salted with words that are labeled "archaic." It is a tombstone announcing the death of a living figure of speech. When I checked my Webster's for the condition of *masculine* and *feminine*, I was glad to see that both still survive, although there was no way to tell if they are merely lingering, brain dead and on a life-support machine.

The bad news is that we have lost our definition of what it means to be men and women; Webster's has something lame to say about a state that is suggestive of being male or female.

Forget that.

The good news is that we can rediscover ourselves and each other before it's time for the embalming fluid.

A few years ago, it was fashionable to "make us the same." Some women went out looking for men who were women, and they just happened to have penises. This prototype was advertised as sensitive and thoughtful and open. It even shed tears, but there was something missing in the excitement department, and after all of about twelve seconds, interest in that androgynous creature started to fade away. Ever since, there's been a question mark hanging over both men and women.

But we'll never find the definition by looking in the wrong places. In neither case does it mean that masculine dominates the feminine; or that one is strong and the other weak. It just means that we are different. Don't forget the old saw that opposites attract. They do, and they make a lot of heat, excitement, and sexual tension in the process. The French word *frisson* catches the deliciousness of it.

The New Dad

The search to rediscover the what and the why of men leads straight back to the function—although that sounds grimly mechanical—of being fathers. In one important sense, we have not changed at all. Our contribution to the reproductive process, aside from stylistic considerations, remains about the same as it has always been. Yet, beyond the sperm fertilizing the egg, men are going about the business of being fathers in a vastly different way.

Men are better fathers than they once were. Even ardent feminists tend to agree that in this area men have made significant improvements. We are more devoted, caring fathers. I think we've seen the fun and fulfillment in becoming fathers. I suppose, to be flippant, taking care of the kids is a lot more enjoyable than cleaning the house. There's more pleasure in bouncing the baby than in scrubbing the kitchen floor.

But getting Dad out of his easy chair and into the child-rearing arena is a dynamic and positive change. As a result, children will fully engage with both parents and be better off because their fathers are actively involved in their lives.

The average guy is cuddling his kids now. I did a *Today*

show story about a school for new fathers in St. Paul, Minnesota. The overwhelming majority of the fathers there were blue-collar guys. They were telephone repairmen, construction workers, truck drivers, etc. We're not talking about Santa Monica or the Upper East Side of Manhattan. And you should have seen them with their babies. They were holding them and hugging them and kissing them; they took the extra effort to go to a school every Saturday morning to learn how to be better fathers—how to change diapers, how to massage the kid, how to be more in touch with the child. They would commiserate, share their feelings, their fears, their apprehensions, about being a new father. These were first time dads, and, as I said, this wasn't the quiche and Chablis crowd—nobody pulled up in a Volvo, I can assure you of that.

Avi Cohen, a TV producer, fits the yuppie stereotype a little more closely because of his job and big-city lifestyle. He's the one who got me interested in the dilemma of the new dad. Avi dutifully went to all the Lamaze classes with his wife; he called them "huff-and-puff sessions." But when the baby was born he felt totally unprepared for what was happening to his life. All the attention was on his wife, on their new son. Avi, as soon as the boy arrived, felt like he was being left out of this family he had helped create.

The poor guy was constantly exhausted; he was walking around the office in a stupor most of the time. It was amazing that he got as much work done as he did. At times you'd hear him ask, half joking and half serious, "What have I gotten myself into?" He was amazed and, I think, angry that fathers are never told what it's going to be like. They're never told anything. Women, mothers, have it drilled into them—you can expect postpartum depression, you can expect, maybe, that you'll shed the weight you gained. Fathers aren't told a thing. Your own father isn't much of a help. It's like some secret masonic order. You can go to school and learn how to tune the engine of your car, but fatherhood is the great mystery of your life, and you learn by doing. No wonder we're all thumbs, full of stupid questions and floundering around. If women start from the premise that men are finally coming out of the dark ages and moving into a renaissance, then maybe we can really start to make progress.

In the end, Avi muddled through his difficult early days of fatherhood. Being a parent, though, is too important to be left to muddling. The schools for new dads, including the Minnesota operation I visited, reflect the interest men like Avi are showing in unraveling the mystery of parenting. They know that being a good father doesn't have anything to do with learning a secret handshake. It starts with a hug.

A bit farther down the road, when the child is out of diapers, there is another level of fathering that men are beginning to participate in with enthusiasm. In a follow-up piece on the "new father," I set out to see whether men were ready to tackle a hands-on parenting role that has traditionally been left to women. I found three men who were actively involved in rearing school-aged children. They juggled busy professional lives with the demands of being "Mister Mom." Cooking, cleaning, supervising homework, chauffeuring, kissing bruised knees, and refereeing squabbles were all in a day's work.

We always hear that pictures are worth a thousand words, but I think it's more like a million. The pictures of those men and their children spoke volumes. Each of the men was daring to do something that his own father had been unable to manage. They were taking the time and the energy and the emotional capital that would have otherwise gone into a career, and investing them into the highest-yield growth fund of them all, a family. And the great thing was that for those guys payday was every day.

Dial *M*—for Masculine

As much as we change, though, men are never going to transform themselves into mothers. And women should ask themselves just how much they want men to change. Do you really want them to be less than masculine?

Lee Eisenberg, the editor of *Esquire*, points out that the ideal man is one who is genuinely and gentlemanly masculine. Not macho—macho is the comic-book version—but masculine. I listened to Lee offer his assessment on a talk show that featured a series of diatribes against men. "The fact is, roles have changed and men no longer accept the stereotype[s], as women do not," he said in response to one of the more outrageous comments. "More and more, men and women are utilizing themselves as a partnership. Whichever of the two does something better, does it. If the man likes to come home and cook because it relaxes him, then he will cook. If the woman is better at making money than the man, she will make more money than the man. A lot of people who I know have come to their new sex roles very naturally and, it seems, very fairly, as though life and marriage were a partnership and not some kind of punishment a woman and a man was sentenced to. And a lot of the images and, if you'll forgive me, the cartoon characters that I think you're dealing with here simply don't exist. . . . There's a major social change going on with men and women."

Men, thanks to the pressure they've been under in recent years, need help in rediscovering their masculinity, digging it out from behind the cartoon caricatures that Lee Eisenberg mentioned. Many of us have forgotten how to be masculine and we drop into macho overdrive, thinking that's the answer. Women compound the problem by using *macho* as an all-purpose buzz word that gets wheeled out whenever a guy does something they don't like. "Oh, don't give me that macho stuff!" What they're talking about is a man's natural and positive masculinity.

A masculine man, to me, is someone who is willing to take a chance and take charge, no matter what other people say or think. He's the guy you can count on in an emergency. All hell is breaking loose and this is the man who says, "Hold it, follks, this is what we're going to do." He's not a bully; he doesn't abuse anyone. He is a take-charge guy, quietly and firmly seizing the moment to get the job done. If women respond to a masculine man, it doesn't mean they are weak or incapable. Why should we stifle another individual's potential to make a contribution?

Making the Irrational Rational

Masculinity—in the best sense of the word—can be very painful. I discovered this dark side of the moon when I researched a story on the impact of rape on the husbands, lovers, sons, and male friends of women who are attacked.

It goes without saying that the rape victim gets first and last call on all the medical and emotional first-aid resources a community can muster. She's been through hell. But the men in her life are going through a trauma of their own.

There is intense anger, bewilderment, and an impulse to do violence. They feel that they have failed to protect the woman they love. These men also need help, and rape crisis centers have found that by reaching out to them, rape victims directly benefit.

For all the changes we've discussed, there is one thing that hasn't changed, and it's what I mean by the pain of masculinity. He wants to kill the rapist, to get back at him, to undo the damage through sheer force and overriding willpower. It's perfectly understandable, but interjecting more violence into a nightmare of violence only harms everyone.

In talking to men who have gone through the experience, they all said they blamed themselves for not being there, even if it was impossible. One guy, a truck driver, was out of town making a delivery. Another was home taking care of the kids while his wife was at a nearby shopping center. As a result, the guilt feelings get all bottled up inside, and if there is an explosion, the relationship can be badly damaged at a time when it should be offering the victim maximum strength and stability.

Often men don't want to have sex with their wives or girlfriends after a rape. Marriages get rocky and sometimes fall apart. There has to be an outlet so that men can talk and cry about the hurt. Irrational feelings must have a means of expression, or those feelings will come out in an irrational, destructive way.

The rape crisis programs have succeeded in convincing some men that it's not good to try to "tough it out." And the guys I met were not the warm, sensitive, fuzzy types: a truck driver, a schoolteacher, and a college-football player. They were willing to change—or at least to try. I don't think it would have happened twenty-five or thirty years ago.

There is a toe in the water, though men will never go as far as women would like. To borrow a line from William Shakespeare, "The fault . . . is not in our stars, but in ourselves." The strengths and weaknesses are so intertwined that they support and reinforce each other in a yin-and-yang combination. Darkness and light; good and bad. That's not to say that nothing changes, for better or worse. The changes come slowly. Otherwise, as men, we risk losing not only our faults but our stars.

CHAPTER SIXTEEN

HAPPILY EVER AFTER

I blame it on Clark Kent. The mild-mannered reporter convinced a couple of generations of young TV viewers that they were supposed to grow up and jump tall buildings in a single bound.

Superman and Superwoman live . . . or at least they try to. "Having it all" is the motto. But the truth is, nobody—nobody—can have it all. Life is a series of trade-offs. You just have to hope that in the end you get more than you gave up.

The price can be a few cents or astronomical. The "Superwoman" and the "Superman" sounded good on paper, but we were sold a bill of goods. It's an impossible dream and it frustrated us. We were tantalized by the prospect of being a superperson. All you have to do is work a little harder, dress a little better, intimidate the other guy a little more effectively—and you live happily ever after. We tried it, many of us are still trying, but it doesn't work.

I think we're slowly coming to our senses. We've learned the hard way. But it doesn't mean men are interested in turning back the clock to the "good old days." First of all, the good old days weren't all that good. Second, the bad new days aren't all that bad. Women have changed to suit the times, and those changes are exciting and rewarding. They are breaking out of the prison of traditional gender roles, but they can still be women. The same goes for men. We are better fathers, lovers, and friends, and the essential man—the solid core—is unchanged.

Sure, there are guys who would love to climb into the time machine and revisit the 1950s, when women knew their place. And there are folks who'd just as soon return to those not-so-thrilling days of yesteryear when we had racially segregated schools and drinking fountains. But they are on the fringes. Real progress has been made in this country. It's not perfect, but we've been moving in the right direction.

One of the reasons I wanted to write this book was to measure the distance we've traveled. It does help to look at the odometer once in a while. Otherwise, all we hear is the constant drumbeat of criticism announcing that men are hopeless and that for every step forward we've taken two steps back. It's the kind of stuff that makes for a self-fulfilling prophesy.

Seduction Strategy

A final item from my notebook: Barbara. A marketing executive who is easily in the top 99 percentile of her profession. We attended a seminar in the Southwest, and during one of the breaks, knowing my specialty and background, Barbara told me that she and her husband do not have a marriage—they've got an affair going. They flirt with each other, work out seduction strategies, and, figuratively (and, I suppose, literally), rub up against each other until they're red-hot.

What could I say? "You've got the ideal marriage" is what I said, and I meant it. She said her husband doesn't care if other men find her attractive, and, in fact, he likes it. Their interest is confirmation that he's got a hell of a woman. The two of them are having a marathon affair. "We get so turned on at times that if we're in the car we pull off the road and make love in the back," she said. "We go off to sleazy hotels just for the fun of it."

To me, Barbara is the real "Superwoman," and her husband is the "Superman." She is extremely successful and so is he. I asked her how her husband reacts to her career. "He tells me to go for it, but to remember that when I come home he's my stage-door lover." They're not trying to have it all. Acquisitiveness, grabbing all the gusto, is not what's happening. Barbara and her husband have changed without changing. They are still man and woman—and making the most of it, hanging on to it, while their professional lives unfold in a way their parents and grandparents could never have imagined.

They've got it all. No, I said I hate the phrase—they've got more because they haven't given up the important things that come with being masculine and feminine.

A Mommy's Boy

Barbara would probably object if I held her up as a role model, so instead I'll offer the prime minister of Norway. A few years ago, Gro Brundtland was kind enough to take time out of her busy schedule to give me a glimpse of how she has reconciled her marriage and private life with a high-powered career in politics.

I don't know what I expected, but I didn't expect such a "together" couple. I was able to bring in my camera crew one morning at breakfast time, and I immediately noticed she was carefully buttering his toast. Now, this is one of Europe's leading crusaders for women's rights. It could have been Madison Avenue–style media manipulation, but the Norwegians really aren't into that kind of thing. I took it as an automatic and unselfconscious gesture.

Both Gro Brundtland and her husband, Arne, are as tough as they come. She leans way to the left politically, and he is an outspoken conservative commentator. Arne doesn't hesitate to take potshots at his wife in the press. And she let's it roll right off her back.

I went through the Norwegian television archives on them; you could spend months screening NBC's footage on the Reagans or George and Barbara Bush, but they're not as into the media age as we are and it only took a couple of hours. I found tape of the Brundtlands at their country home outside Oslo. He is in the foreground chopping wood while she's chatting with reporters off to the side. It was as if I were watching a Rose Garden news conference with this guy blithely splitting kindling. Arne was unabashedly doing his thing while his wife did hers.

In subsequent interviews, both of them acknowledged that a lot of the chemistry between them is due to the success of their individual careers. There isn't anything lopsided about the relationship. He doesn't feel that he is living in her shadow, or vice versa. They take a lot of pride in each other's accomplishments. I think that's where a lot of the tranquillity in their private life comes from.

The prime minister made an interesting point about Arne's background. She said that his mother had been a distinguished physician and that, as a result, being married to a woman with a professional career is no big deal to him. She suggested that in Norway women have historically had access to the top rungs of the professional ladder.

I wonder if that isn't a portent of our future. As American women climb that ladder, American men—the sons of physicians, like Arne Brundtland—will take it as a matter of course when they end up married to the president of a Fortune 500 corporation or the president of the United States.

And maybe the future is now. There are plenty of couples like the Brundtlands. Sally Jessy Raphaël and her husband, Karl Sunderland, come to mind immediately. She is the star with her own television talk show, and he is her business manager. They work together beautifully without any hang-ups.

Sure, Sally is a star with a huge salary. She is the queen, but he is the prime minister, responsible for administering the empire. Karl is one ferocious watchdog when Sally's interests are at stake. He is not threatened by her success—on the contrary—and she is not threatened when those "masculine tendencies" are brought to bear on her behalf. They're partners.

I like that word; it has a good, solid feel—*partners*.

Ideals and Bad Deals

Partnerships are fine for Gro Brundtland and Sally Jessy Raphaël, but you shouldn't set out to form a partnership with a man if that's not what you want. We've been smothered in role models: the ideal man, the ideal woman, the ideal couple. Chasing after those ideals can be a fool's game if the ideal isn't ideal for you.

Earlier, I told you about the basic simplicity of men,

and that simplicity has probably shielded them from some of the good and bad fashions in role models. We're still working off of John Wayne, and he stepped right out of a Zane Grey novel. Grey was updating Daniel Boone.

The way we dress says a lot about our attitudes. Men and women are bombarded by sophisticated advertising campaigns for the latest jeans, sweaters, raincoats—you name it. Despite it all, men are still wearing the same old blue blazers, penny loafers, and button-down shirts. Some men are a little more tuned in to the fashion scene, but most stay with the tried and true.

For men, fashion trickles down from the top. We tend to dress like the boss. When Ed, who sells computer disk drives, got a news sales manager from California, one of his savvy customers predicted that within weeks the company's marketing people would be wearing gold Rolex watches and wire-rim aviator glasses and driving expensive European cars. Ed laughed. He kept time with a battered vintage Omega and there had never been anything other than Detroit iron in his garage.

You can guess the postscript on this story—Ed's into the Rolex, the Volvo, and the wire rims.

Fashion accessories—and I suppose a car can be a fashion accessory—became important during the 1980s, when the Rodeo Drive style of displaying one's wealth and success was set by the Reagan White House.

But there is always a practical side to men's fashion: If red suspenders are good for business, go for it.

And speaking of red suspenders, that's one fashion trend that trickled up before it trickled down. Like a pirate's black eye patch, the suspenders became a symbol of a swashbuckling younger generation of brokers and entrepreneurs. Their elders saw them coming, and in a flash the only belt to be found in most New York executive offices was in a bottle of Beefeater's gin.

His and Hers Tool Chests

A man's clothes are tools of his trade. As tools, like a hammer and a screwdriver, the things he wears are basic. Women spend a lot of money coordinating the color of their eye shadow with their shoes and handbags, but men could care less. I'm not saying you should clear off your makeup table and wear sackcloth. Your interest in such things reflects your complexity as a woman. His lack of interest reflects his simplicity as a man.

This complexity-simplicity conflict bumps up against things like role models and creates tension between men and women. When the media throws up a new role model, like the Huxtables in *The Cosby Show*, it can create a desire to achieve that ideal. But when men are slow to respond —Daniel Boone Huxtable? Cliff Wayne? Zane Cosby?— there's trouble. Complexity and simplicity clash.

What I'm saying is that in many cases men aren't paying attention to the same things that women focus on, and they don't react in the same way. Consequently, they are slower to change.

And I think I'll stop right here without saying whether I think that slowness is good or bad. You have to decide on that.

The Uses of Power

There are other decisions to be made as well. The reason for this book is to provide you with information about men on which you can base those important decisions. And no one else can make them but you.

It all comes down to power. If you don't use it, he will. Make that power work for you. Recognize, though, that power is a burden. Working out an agenda for a relationship, articulating the priorities and sticking to them, does not make for carefree fun. Understanding that a guy is operating with a different commitment timetable and waiting for him to meet you halfway isn't a lot of laughs. But the choice is power or powerlessness.

Men use power on their own behalf. They've always done it and always will. But I'm not saying that you must seize his power. Leave the coup d'état business to the Argentines. Plug into the power generated by the nuclear material of your own femininity.

Dirty Words and Last Words

I'm an optimist, and I feel good about where we are headed. There's a balance taking hold. The best of both worlds—the masculine and feminine worlds—is coming together. It seemed for a while that we were in danger of turning away from ourselves as men and women by trying to create a half-and-half hybrid. But masculine men and feminine women are getting a new lease on life. For one thing, the terms *masculine* and *feminine*, which I have used throughout this book, aren't dirty words anymore.

At the same time, the new ideas that have come along in the last twenty-five years are still making sparks. We haven't tried to go back to square one, where men are men and women are barefoot and pregnant. Good things are happening that would have been unthinkable a generation ago.

Men and women are learning. We're learning what we like and dislike about each other. We're learning what to change and when to leave well enough alone. We're learning that men and women are different, and that those differences have a magnetic power to draw us toward love, passion, and fulfillment.

Claude and Pena found all of that and more. Their affair started in Paris. He is French, she's Italian. Neither one spoke the other's native language. Claude's English is excellent; Pena could make it through a copy of *People* magazine but not *The Atlantic*. As they made love that first night, in a small hotel on the Left Bank, Pena, swept toward orgasm, cried out, "I'm . . . I'm arriving . . . I'm arriving . . ."

And she was arriving. Claude and Pena, men and women, are arriving—together—despite different languages, timetables, and priorities. The road has plenty of ruts and potholes, yet we are disproving those who said, "You can't get there from here." We're arriving.